AF493308

Swirling Symmetry

Thoughts and Images
Mathematics, Motion & Pattern

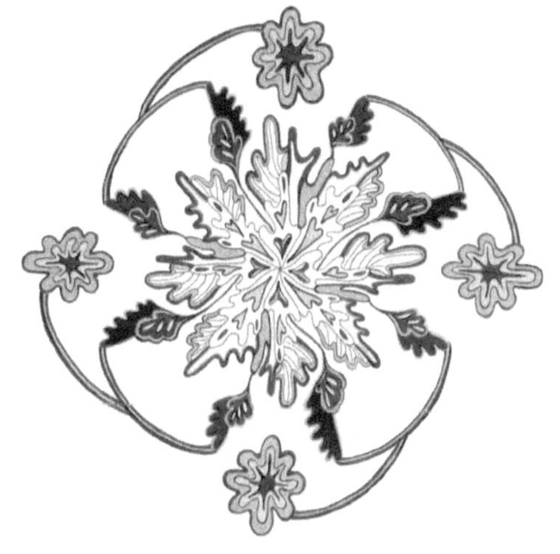

Sandra DeLozier Coleman

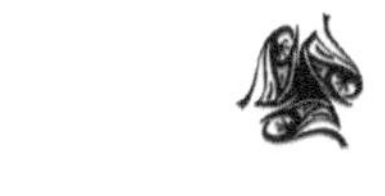

Bohannon Hall Press

Copyright © 2022 by Sandra DeLozier Coleman
All rights reserved
Printed in the United States of America

Algorithmic art © by Sandra DeLozier Coleman
Cover design by Sandra DeLozier Coleman
Sculpture images courtesy of Helaman Ferguson
Bird Illustrations by Sarah Robin Coleman

Library of Congress Control Number: 2022915444

Publisher's Cataloging-in-Publication Data

Coleman, Sandra DeLozier, 1949-
    Swirling Symmetry: Thoughts and Images Mathematics Motion &
    Pattern / by Sandra DeLozier Coleman ; illustrated by Sandra DeLozier
    Coleman, Sarah Robin Coleman and sculpture images courtesy of
    Helaman Ferguson.
    Niceville, FL: Bohannon Hall Press, 2022.
    164 p.: illustrations ; 23 cm.
    First edition.

1. Coleman, Sandra DeLozier -- Poetry. 2. Mathematics – Poetry. I. Title. II.
Coleman, Sarah Robin, 1977- III. Ferguson, Helaman.
PS3603.044 S95 2022   LC2022915444

ISBN 979-8-9850298-6-4 (softcover)
ISBN 979-8-9850298-3-3 (hardcover)

Published by Bohannon Hall Press

*To my mother
who pondered and discussed non-trivial questions
all her life, drawing on manifold resources
in her limitless quest for Truth*

Table of Contents

Introduction

It was in the middle of a college chemistry class that I found myself being distracted from the words coming from the stage as a professor tried to teach a chemistry lesson to me and my hundred or so classmates. An idea talked about in calculus class earlier that day was sending my thoughts off in a different direction. An English-class assignment to write a structured poem may have led me to try to force the thoughts about higher dimensions that were occupying my mind into patterned rhyme. I wrote the poem I called *The Calculus* by the end of class – the first of many math and physics-based thoughts to be framed in rhyme and patterned drawings over the next many years.

To rhyme or not to rhyme? That has almost become an answered question, with the answer seemingly falling on the side of *not,* or even *never.* My use and love of pattern – which includes rhyme, symmetry and analysis of what it is about a certain shape, or set of words, that is, to me, appealing – sometimes has me feeling very much the way I felt as a young girl, who pursued a love for mathematics at a time when many people harbored the thought that girls *don't,* or even, *can't* do math. I suppose I have always been a bit of a non-conformist.

Despite mountains of discouragement, I continued to study math just because I loved to study math. I write in rhyme, because I love to write in rhyme. The other ninety percent of my poems are not based on math or physics – unless you've come to believe that everything is based on math or physics – but almost all of my poems rhyme. There is an element involved in writing the clearly-math-based poems that makes them doubly pleasant to create, because they involve a challenging call for adherence to both form and fact.

The physics-based poems are so obviously written from an interested layman's point of view that I would not dare to say they lay out facts. The poems are colored by ideas about the nature of the physical universe that I have encountered through reading, but have not yet fully explored. The references are not based on knowledge gained through intensive academic study, but rather, on ideas that have intrigued me and sparked my imagination. Hopefully, the poems will inspire at least a few readers to delve deeper into their basis in scientific thought.

For many years I have been sharing plans for this book of patterned words and art in conversations with friends and acquaintances. I have tried to dispel any dismissive thoughts that the collection is intended only for people who have studied math or physics. I can make a good case for a broader audience by reciting just a few poems. When listeners respond by writing down the book title with clear plans to read the full set, I feel confident that they will enjoy the reading, even if they are among the group of people quick to say that they are not good at, or never liked, math. While it *is true* that there are some poems for which only mathematicians can be an appreciative audience, for the most part, the ideas considered are of interest to us all.

Exploring a collection of patterned poems and images can create a feeling of peace and calm, not unlike the feeling that comes from observing pattern in nature. When used to express ideas on math and physics, patterned words can have the emotional effect of making it seem as though everything has its proper place in this complicated universe. It can be very nice to have a book of poems to turn to on days when events in the world around us seem to be jarringly chaotic.

Readers will discover here poems referencing math concepts from zero to infinity and physics concepts like event horizons, black holes, and parallel universes. Some poems can be used as teaching tools. Some inspire questions or defend the right to ask questions. Others give answers so precise that they include equations presented in rhyming mathematical notation. Still others present arguments for why some of the greatest of all questions must forever remain unanswered.

The drawings that have been in Bridges Mathematical Art exhibitions are accompanied by the words I originally used to describe them. Some explain the effect on my spirit of the process of creating symmetrical images without the use of computer technology or measuring devices. It is impossible to have a mind racing with scattered or unpleasant thoughts while creating symmetry in ink.

There are many references to the works of mathematical sculptor, Helaman Ferguson. I have written poems about all of the sculptures in the book, *Helaman Ferguson, Mathematics in Stone and Bronze*. Several of these have been presented at math conferences or previously published in math journals with images. Some poems were inspired by conversations with Helaman on mathematical topics or on his plans for more sculptures.

Near the end of the book, there is a set of poems related to works of well-known, widely-admired poets whose poems vary greatly in form. In an effort to better understand the role of pattern, or lack thereof, in the framing of their words, I have composed several analogous poems that reflect my own thoughts in poems clearly based on their works. This imitative form of writing has benefits that are similar to the benefits apprentice artists experience in trying to duplicate the works of the great masters. The apprentices develop sensitivities and skills as they work that can influence, and possibly improve, their own creations. In a similar way, a poet can explore the effects of pattern and other poetic elements through the effort of studying and copying master poets.

In playful response to a poet friend's ideas on *never-rhyme*, a pair of poems, *A Lass, Alas* and *A Caddish Lad*, carry rhyme to humorous extreme. In both, nearly every other word rhymes. Imagine the poems being sung like Irish drinking songs. I do sing the first one often to amuse friends, but I have to ask them to stretch their imaginations to a see me as a man in a pub who is warning a newcomer to town about the woman whose beauty and song are bewitching him from across room!

The last poem is a fairytale ballad about a two-headed giant. It extols the benefits of employing left and right-brain powers in harmony. My husband and I once attended a friend's Halloween party dressed as such a giant of two minds. We wore a *shared* costume. We peered out from inside two papier-mâché heads – think Einstein and Clark Gable – each wearing a single pant leg that covered two legs and one big, black, papier-mâché shoe that covered two feet – open on the bottom to allow us to walk with fairly good coordination. Papier-mâché hands protruded from the sleeves of the gigantic upper part of the costume, which was split down the middle with the two sides joined using Velcro, so that we could separate if one should need to go anywhere without the other. Our costume was a hit with our creative friends and the party was much, much fun!

The acknowledgements for this book should list all of the sources of inspiration, but the list would be very, very long. A few people deserve a special note. Helaman Ferguson and Claire Ferguson through their friendship and their book, *Helaman Ferguson: Mathematics in Stone and Bronze*, have inspired over thirty poems, a few of which are included here. Jesse Purifoy's 1971 topology class with its consideration of Georg Cantor's work on the theory of infinite sets inspired three. John Konvalina's 1986 homework assignments in combinatorics, analysis, and modern geometry inspired several. Our subsequent friendship inspired many more. Thomas Banchoff's *Beyond the Third Dimension: Geometry, Computer Graphics, and Higher Dimensions* led to poems about hypercubes. The art and writings of M. C. Escher are behind a few poems. Poems related to fractals were inspired by Benoit B. Mandelbrot, beginning with *The Fractal Geometry of Nature*. Ideas in the many math and physics trade books I read during the thirteen years I served as Book Review Editor for *The AMATYC Review* color many of the poems. The imitation poems are based on famous poems by Wallace Stevens, Elizabeth Barrett Browning, Rainer Maria Rilke, John Keats, William Wordsworth, and Clement Clarke Moore.

The poet has only to perceive that which others do not perceive,
to look deeper than others look.
The mathematician must do the same thing.

Sofia Kovalevskaya (1850-1891)

THE CALCULUS

MANDELBROT SET

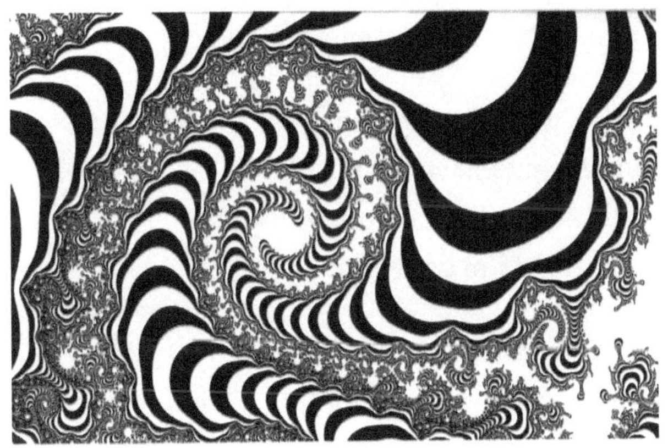

The Cheshire Cat of Mathematics grins
and tempts the curious Alice to begin
to trace his smile, the outline of his face.
He poses questions. She in turn inquires
about his wondrous nature and aspires
to know the laws supporting him in space.
He answers not, but staring in her eyes,
as though he knows she half believes he lies,
begins to dwindle, disappear, erase,
'til not a trace of cat or smile remains
to thank the careful Alice for her pains.
Alone she stands and scans the empty night,
seeking threads of insight out of sight,
in simple three dimensions seeking proof
of what her mind's eye saw
and knows is truth.

What does more to make me me –
what I am or what I see?
Am I not mostly empty space,
where moving quarks create a face?

But, ah! The motion I perceive!
My mind would have me to believe
that there is really something there.
But is there, if I'm unaware?

My world revolves around my eyes.
Without my mind the whole thing dies.
Why should this be a shameful view?
Your world revolves around you, too!

We're both just particles of dust
in motion – motion is a must –
and mind – or should I call it soul –
which tricks us into feeling whole.

Near Sighted

In a body so confining –
so confined by Space and Time –
is a spirit ever pining
for what never can be mine.
Truths elusive lie beyond me –
for my body cannot hope
to comprehend realities
that lie beyond its scope.

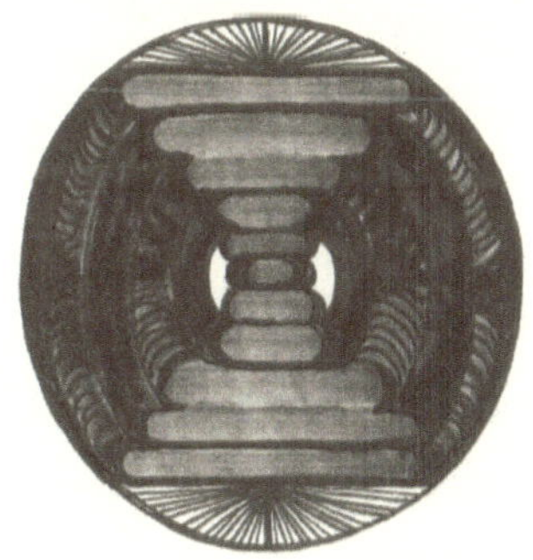

REALITY

Is this water really pink,
because I see it so?
To those same eyes that see it now,
'twas blue an hour ago!

How much does my perception count,
when counting what is real?
How much of life is what we sense?
How much just what we feel?

What does it mean to really know?
And who decides what's true,
when now the water's clearly pink,
which once was clearly blue?

The water's neither pink nor blue,
but clear enough to see right through.
I wonder how much else we spy
is just a mirror of the sky.

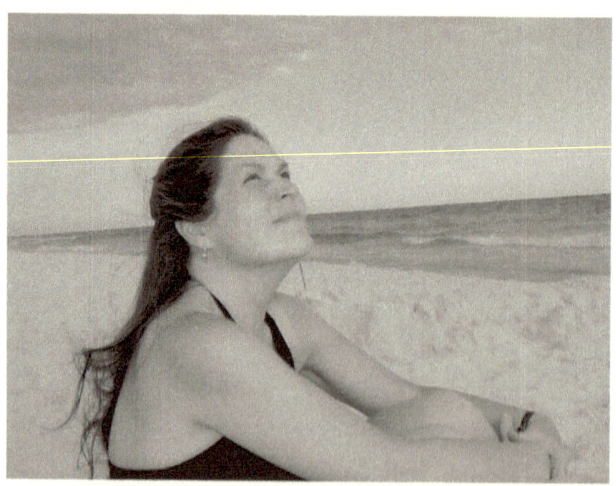

BICYCLE RIDE

If I view the flower on my left,
the other side is missed.
As far as my world is concerned
the right does not exist.
I cannot see two ways at once
at any given time.
My bodily experience
thus limits what is mine.
And yet a part of me believes
in things I neither see
nor yet in any way perceive
with sensuality.

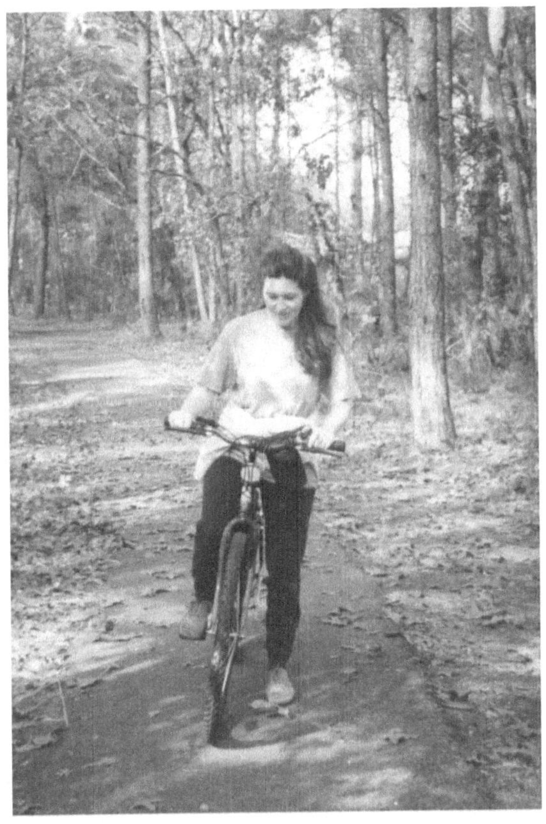

LINKED

A man inquired of the Universe,
what is Truth and why is it so,
and is it a blessing or a curse,
knowing how much we cannot know?

The Universe said to the questing man,
or, at least, he thought he clearly heard,
that each new thing since time began
has from what went before emerged.

Nothing exists not intertwined
with everything else that also is,
and Truth we foolishly define
unless our Truths consider this.

It's not that there's no Absolute,
but it is foolishness to think
to know a thing beyond dispute
and not consider every link.

Our Truths we seek to simplify,
but each reduction adds more thread,
more links that just intensify,
the great already-tangled web.

It's neither a blessing nor a curse,
that nothing can be completely known.
We simply cannot now reverse
the paths by which our Truths have grown.

I love the tangle and the ties
connecting you and them and I –
the links among all living souls
that make the world a changing whole.
This web we cannot well confine
to anything that words define.
Thus, all the Truths that we explore
are chaos we cannot ignore,
but, even so, cannot contain
in any box that is too plain.

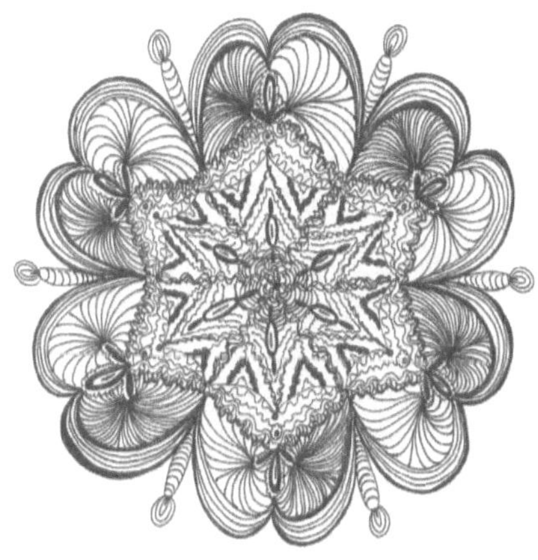

TACKLING TANGLES

When I can't pull a tangle from my hair,
though I've tried my best to pull from every angle,
I don't give up or wallow in despair!
I just start pulling hair out of the tangle!

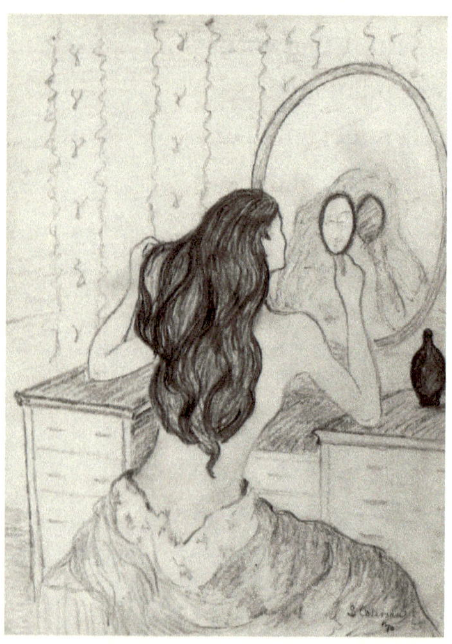

I cannot go beyond myself
to see me as I am,
though I may surely see all else
more clearly than I can
define, or see, the view of me
the outer world perceives –
a view reflecting, endlessly,
whatever it receives.

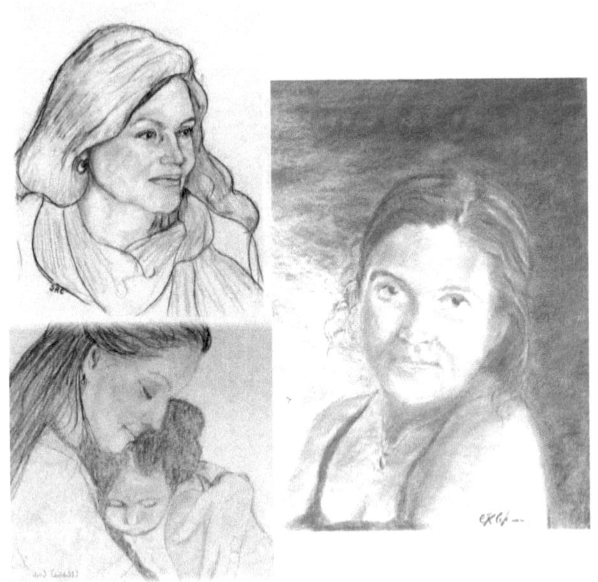

THE POET IN THE EYES OF HER FAMILY

Can we have thoughts completely free
of learned and taught reality?
In physics, or in any field,
might there be more to what is real
than words allow us to conceive?
Do words confine, perhaps deceive?
Forced to connect all we observe
to what we can describe with words,
do words so link us to the past
that Truth is now beyond our grasp?

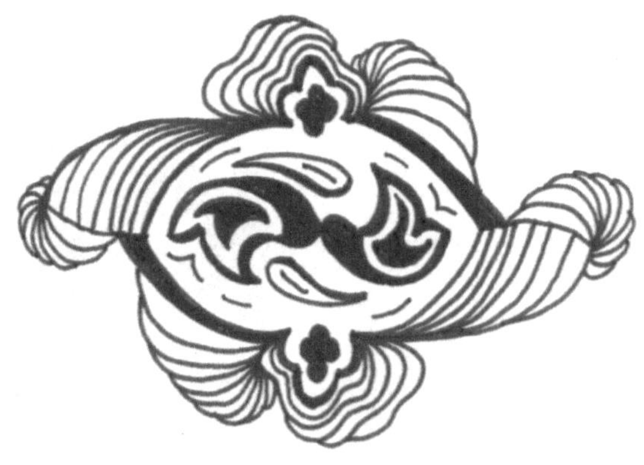

A pity we have to think in words
and cannot let them go,
for often what we say we think
is less than what we know.

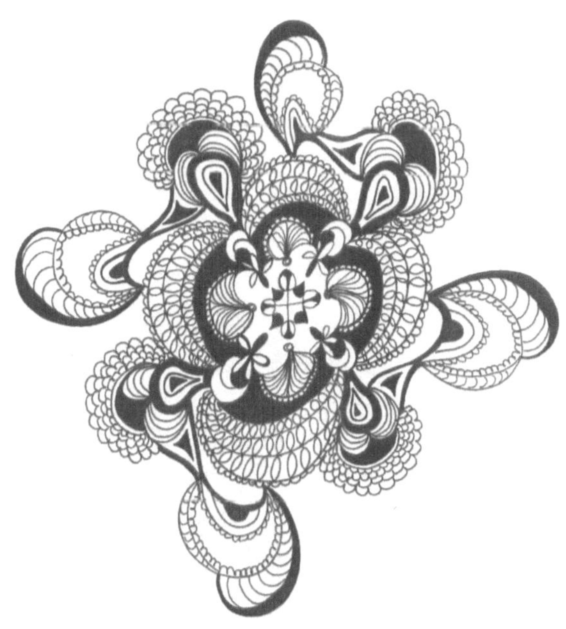

What would it mean to you, to me,
if more should exist than we can see,
if all of the Truths to which we're blind
had no way to enter the human mind?
Could reason allow us to receive
Truths that our sense cannot perceive?
Or are we forever doomed to see
only our small reality?
Of all of the possible working worlds,
is the limited one we see unfurled
just that with which our minds align –
reality of our own design?

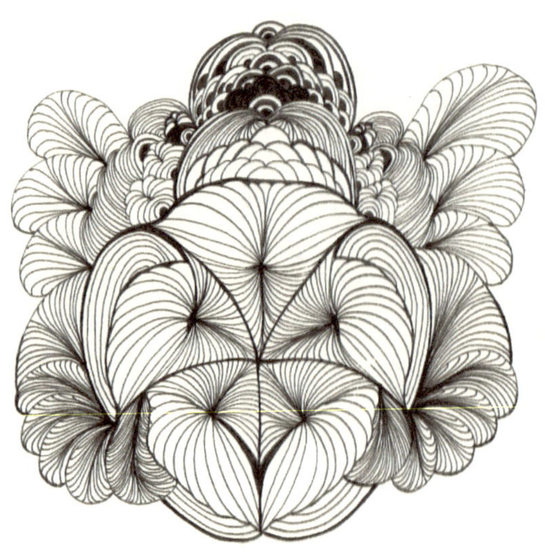

NOTHING NOT MOTION

If motion should decide to stop,
then earth and sea and sky
would neither differ nor exist;
nor, yet, would you, nor I.

If motion had a quarrel with time,
and each went separate ways,
there'd be no here and now –
nor then – nor any other place!

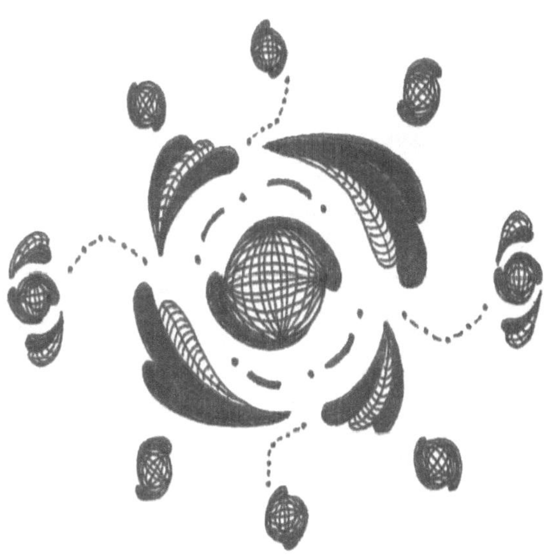

A sculpture made of clay I saw
they called a horned wild sphere.
Though nothing like a sphere at all,
its wildness was quite clear.
In infinite bifurcations
it besought eternity,
and I saw a clear relation
to the wilder side of me.
Arms ever reaching higher
to a world beyond its sphere,
torn by bifurcate desires
never satisfied, I fear.

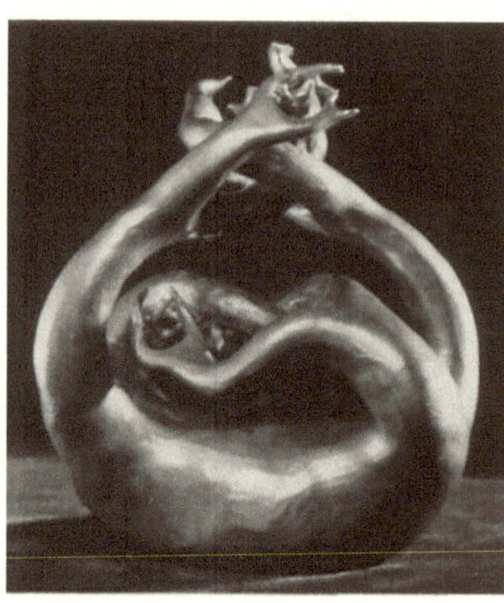

ALEXANDER'S HORNED WILD
SPHERE
Helaman Ferguson, 1985
printed with his permission

CONTINUUM

Good – bad
Sane – mad
Wrong – right
Day – night
In between,
some have seen
people, poems,
poets, schemes
ideas, reasons,
sunsets, dreams.

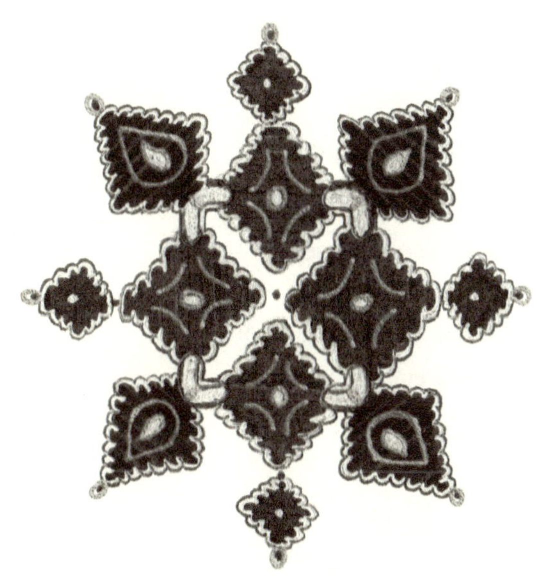

I did not see the sun today.
'twas gone before I came.
Its coral card above the sea
said it would call again.

The sunset hid itself today
behind a cloud of mist.
I did not see the ocean blush,
when by the sun 'twas kissed.

Today the sun turned crimson red
before it said good-bye
and wrapped itself in purple robes
it borrowed from the sky.

The sun was slow to leave today.
It hung above the sea
until the moon rose in the east
to say, "It's time for me!"

Today the sun so hid itself
I scarcely saw it pass,
but knew that it had tiptoed out
when darkness came at last.

Today the sunlight fell in rays
like fingers of a hand
which timidly had opened up
and dared to touch the land.

The sunset that I saw today
could make me heaven regret,
if it be true that there the sun
shall neither rise nor set.

HEAVEN

What in the world must heaven be like?
I'm glad I don't have to decide!
For what's heaven to one
might not be to some,
and it's hell when two heavens collide!

What in the world must heaven be like?
If some people could have their own way,
there would just be a few
of the people they knew,
and the rest would be far, far away.

What in the world must heaven be like?
In the current, most popular view,
we'd all have our health
and no lack of wealth,
but then what on earth would we do?

What in the world must heaven be like?
Perhaps it's a state of the mind,
and we carry within
our beginning and end,
and whatever we look for we find.

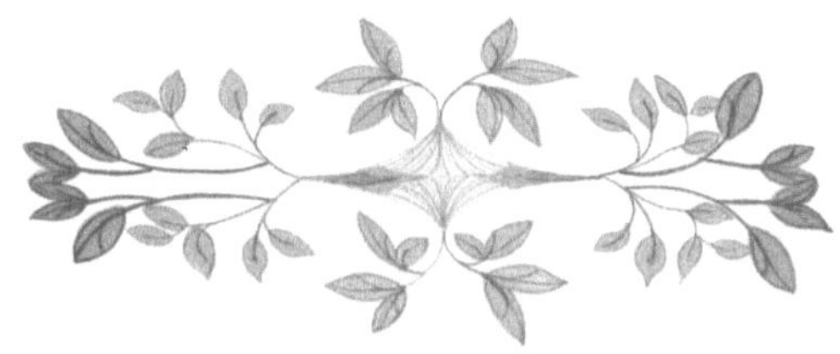

I just began to understand today
the multitude of paths a traveler may
elect to take to work his winding way
from (2, 11, 1) to (15, 13, 7).

I calculate within that tiny space
five million plus distinct paths he may trace,
all headed for one point in Euclid's space!
How many more the paths that lead to heaven!

$$\frac{[(15-2) + (13-11) + (7-1)]!}{(15-2)! \ (13-11)! \ (7-1)!} = \frac{(13 + 2 + 6)!}{13! \ 2! \ 6!} = 5{,}687{,}720$$

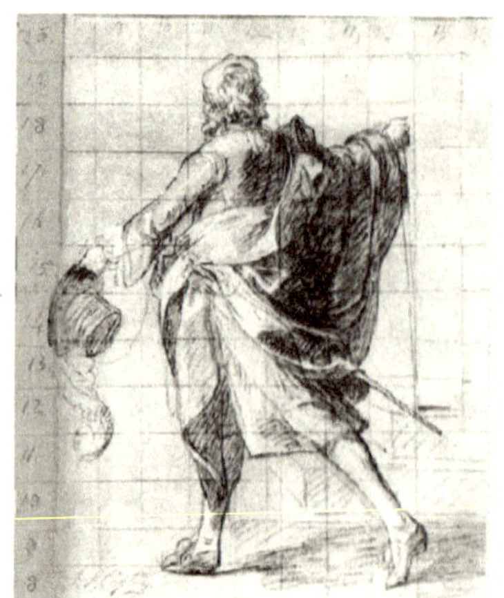

JOHN SINGLETON COPLEY (1738-1815)

THE ROAD TO HEAVEN

The road to heaven's long and steep
and sometimes hard to find.
Though on the pathway I would keep,
it's slippery at times.
Sometimes I fear I've lost my way
or have not yet begun.
At other times I dare not say
my path's the only one.
Perhaps down many thousand paths
our wandering souls must roam,
until we find ourselves at last
no longer far from home.

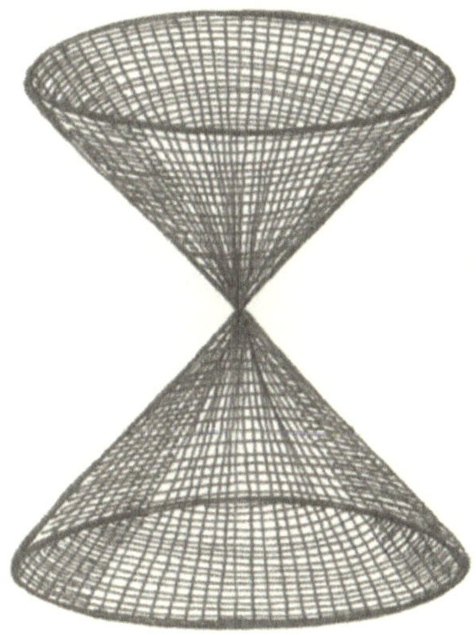

I am full of questions,
as I have always been,
ignoring all suggestion
that questioning is sin.
That notion is so human,
so clearly based on fear,
that, that we should ignore it,
is unquestionably clear.

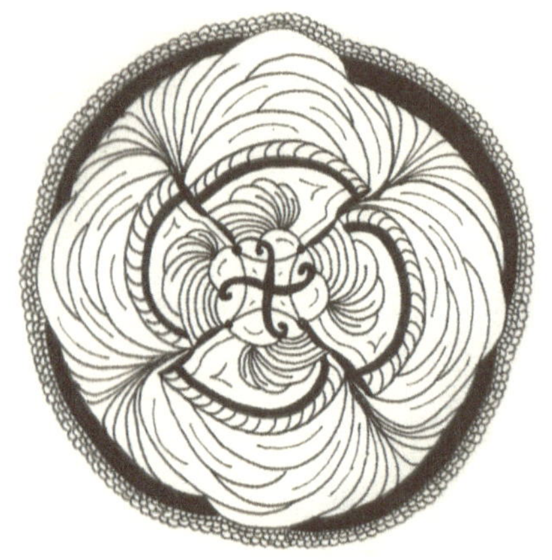

It's been days now since the water's edge
was empty but for me.
It's good to have it to myself again –
to hear the breeze rush by my head
with secrets from the sea
that lonely hearts alone can understand.
The sea is saying, "Life is fleet,
eternity is long,
but when the two are one then there is bliss."
It's only when no one but me
can hear the ocean's song,
I hear it whisper simple truths like this.

If nothing exists we cannot see,
should we conclude stars come to be
the moment that telescopically
they enter the stellar registry,
or say we've made those things so small
that, before lens, were not at all?

That things now known, or thought, to be,
were veiled for most of history,
suggests, it's foolish to deny
that more exists than we can spy,
in micro and in cosmic realms,
and likely in between, as well.

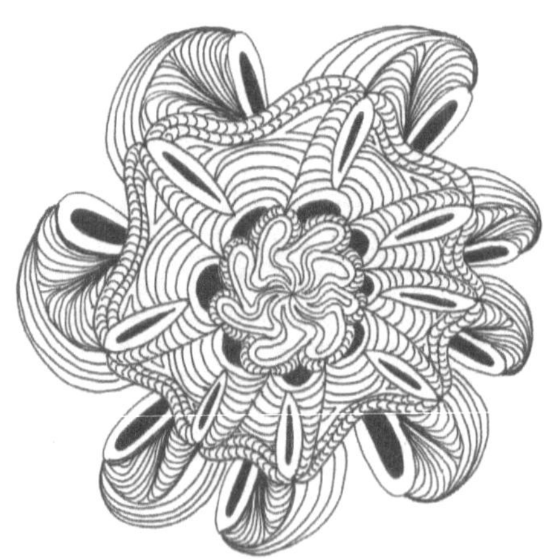

How do we dare to think of things
not handed down as Truths,
when Truths are handed down to us
defying need for proof?

Some, well-established long ago
by councils counted wise,
we've difficulty letting go.
We dare not call them lies.

Good men have told us for so long
what good men must believe,
it does no good to say they're wrong,
much less that they deceive.

How many forward-thinking men
were burnt upon a stake
for pointing out that, now and then,
good men have made mistakes?

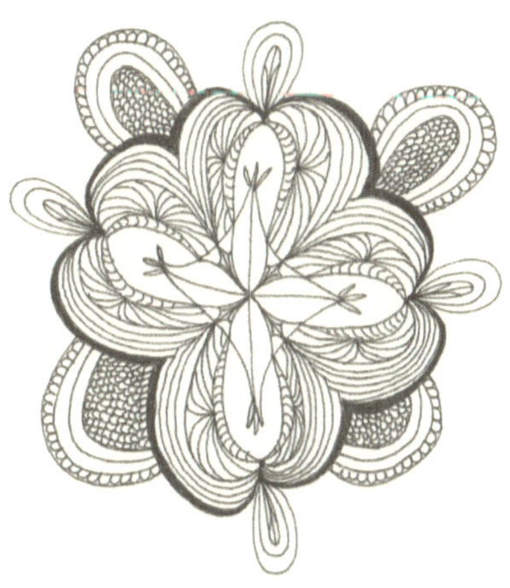

My algorithmic designs are generally drawn freehand without the aid of measuring devices or preliminary sketches. From points dividing an imagined circle into approximately equal parts, repeated steps lead to approximations of rotational symmetries. In this particular design, at one point in the drawing process, I made use of a circular object with a hole in the center to assess and adjust the circularity. The points between the center and the circle's edge and beyond were all estimated, resulting in variations in the sizes and shapes of related areas in the drawing. It is interesting that although corresponding areas are not actually congruent, there is "at a glance" symmetry based on elements that are invariant in the design.

At an art show a few years ago, I was encouraged to demonstrate the process of creating an algorithmic design like this one. I was delighted to find that my booth attracted a large number of children who seemed eager to try to create designs of their own. The question that arose most often as they watched me drawing in ink was, "What if you make a mistake?" It always brought a satisfied nod when I replied that this was one expression of mathematics where it is ok to make mistakes, as long as the mathematical artist makes the same mistake again and again and again!

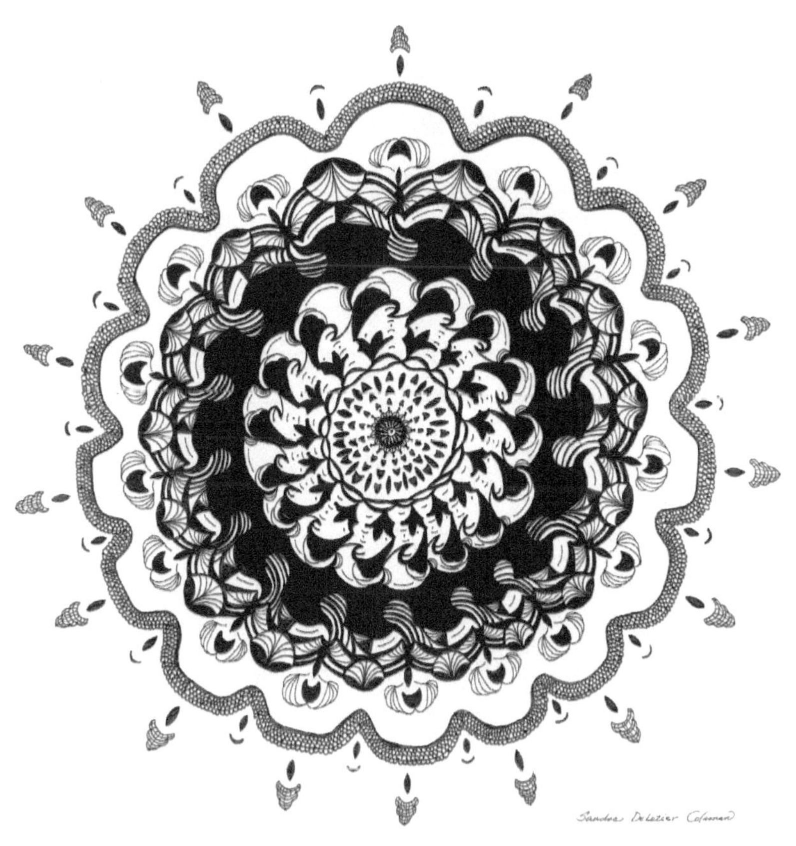

SYMMETRIC EMANATION

21" X 25"
Ink on Paper
2013

Ten to the eleventh stars for every galaxy.
Ten to the eleventh galaxies.
Ten to the twenty-second stars – more than we'll ever see.
How did such jewels of wonder come to be?

Gazing as far as our tools allow
into a sea of starry clouds,
seeing the past from here and now,
how can we help but wonder how?

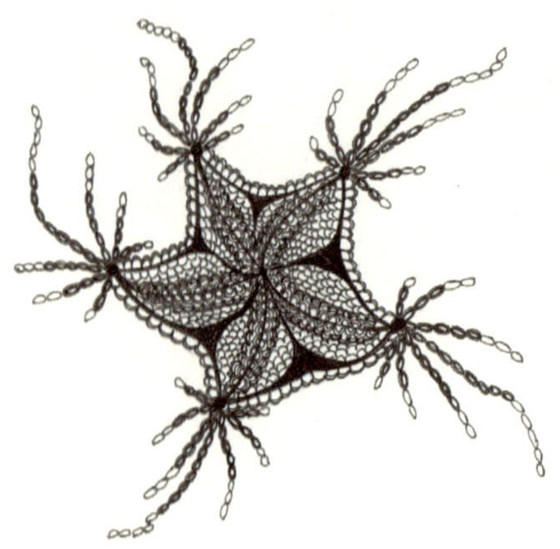

The speed with which a galaxy recedes or runs from us,
our scientists just recently have reckoned.
That which is furthest out we see as leaving in a rush
of 2000+ km/sec.
V. M. Slipher found that 36 he viewed recede at speeds
proportional to their distance from our sun,
but 5 among the ones he saw approach and don't recede.
We have 5 friends among the 41.

Two Sundays were enough it seems
to understand full well
why Emily deems parting
taste of heaven – glut of hell.

Two Sundays so dissimilar,
yet, oddly, in one place,
where once you dared to show your heart,
where once you hid your face.

Two Sundays I would live again,
if heaven would be so kind.
The second would be worth the pain,
the first again to find.

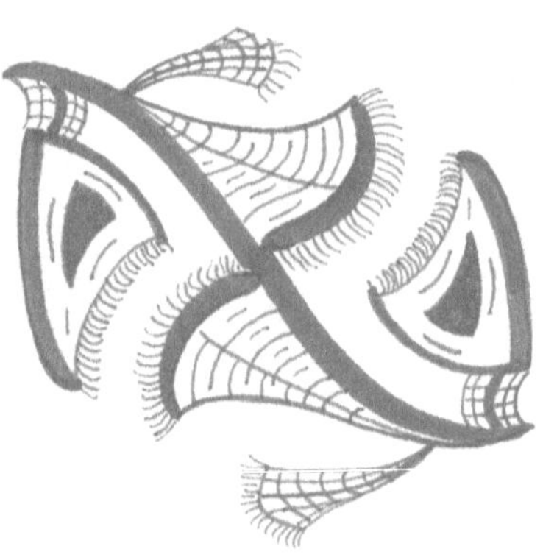

AFTERMATH

The breeze is still here, as always.
The sea waves still come and go.
The sun on the sea still sparkles.
The sand's still as white as snow.
Yet, so much has changed, it's hard to
believe this the place I know,
except for the grass by the water,
which just seems to grow and grow.

The trees that I loved have fallen.
The boardwalk has disappeared.
Though birds, as before, are calling,
there's no place to sit and hear.
For this place that I loved, I'm disheartened
at what it's become this year,
and it tears at my soul to part with
the heaven that once was here.

This debris and destruction so senseless,
every place I direct my eyes,
tell me beauty is weak and defenseless
when the winds blow and waters rise.
Here my thoughts and my feelings were tenderest,
where the sea sang me lullabies.
But the cycles of life are endless,
full of meetings and sad goodbyes.

It was such a little thing,
this friendship that we shared.
But life is full of little things
of which we're unaware –
until we find them missing,
and, then missing them, we find,
it's hard to fill with anything
the space they left behind.

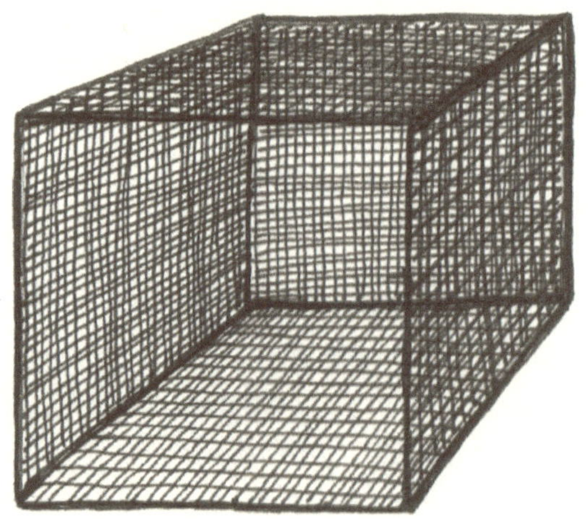

A friend told me
he'd heard the sea
inspires poetic thought,
because it fills
our logic cells
with little food for thought.
We have to stress
creativeness
to think beside the sea.
Perhaps that's why
it's here that I
am writing poetry.

Poetry, art and mathematics present common aspects to me. In the realm of poetry, I find rhyme and rhythm to be as satisfying as free verse and in art I find the pattern and repetition of symmetrical drawing to be as calming as meditation. In both, making the choice to define a pattern and then to adhere to the plan once begun, presents just enough of a challenge to force my mind to tune out any unpleasant clamoring of racing thoughts and for a time to let go, absorbed in the flow of the moment. The feeling is not so very different from the feeling of satisfaction that comes from completing a proof or from changing the forms of certain equations so that we can quickly analyze the geometric characteristics of the functions.

SUSURRUS is a delicate circle of symmetry intending to capture the feather-like murmuring sound, the whispering soft repetition of waves washing over a shore, of wind moving blossoming branches, of seagulls at once taking flight.

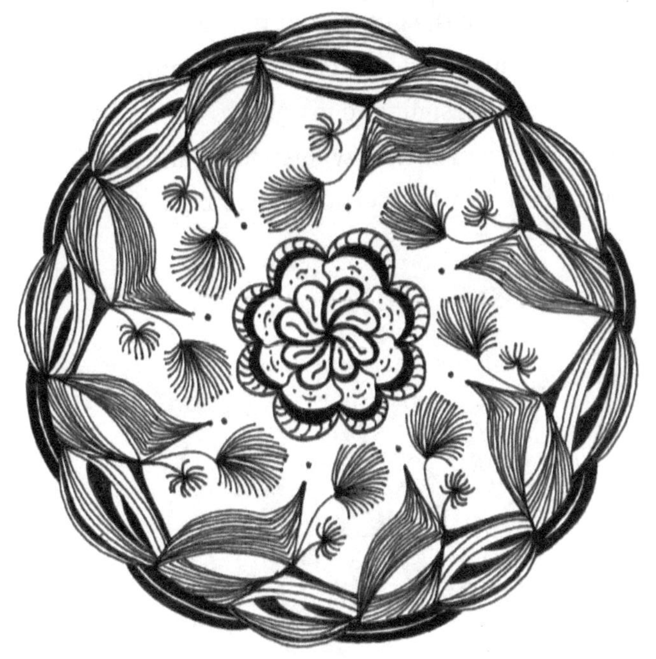

SUSURRUS
12" x 14"
Ink on paper
2015

I feel that I could trust you with my eyes.
So deep the tender bond between us lies
that, were you blind and I possessed of sight,
I could forego the gift, accept perpetual night,
and yield my precious vision to your mind,
which, having sight and insight, so would find
such beauty in each new-seen form and line,
I should prefer your vision to be mine.

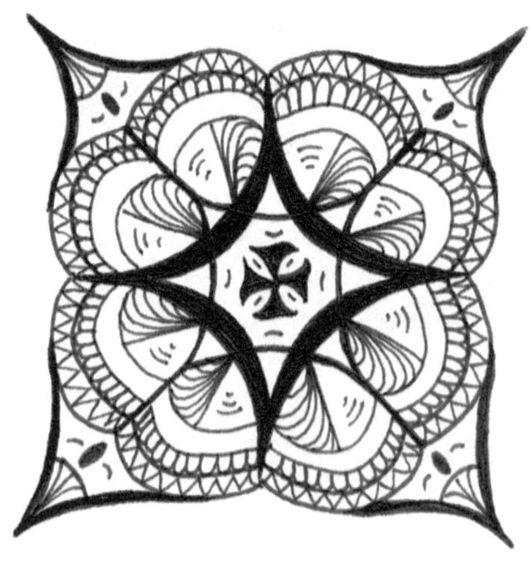

Self-similarity is more profound
in shapes that are polygonal or round.
But, none-the-less, I think you will agree
that lines exhibit similarity.

Beginning at some arbitrary source,
extending on a straight, unbending course,
one line is like another, if it ends,
regardless of the distance it extends.

But it's a very different entity –
a line extending to infinity.

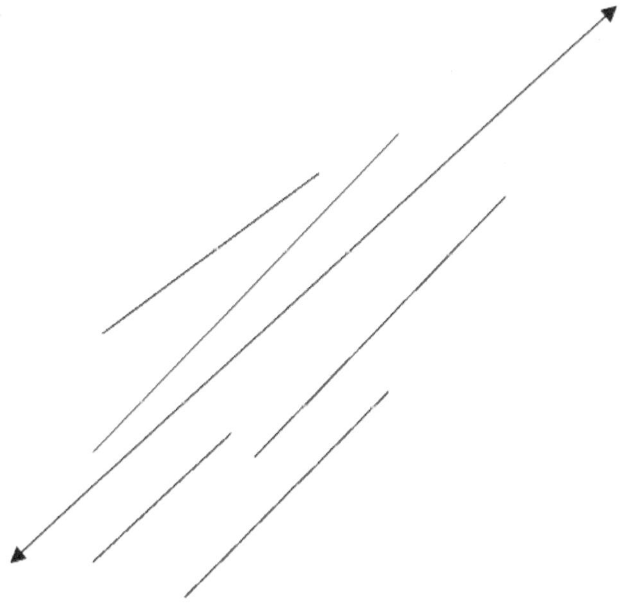

Each life's a great circle upon a great sphere.
Each birth date determines an origin year.
To the right lies each future, while each person's past
extends to the left somehow out of his grasp.
We live out the units of life on a line,
confined to our space and compelled through our time.
We strive and we struggle our paths to transcend
'til we meet at the place of Beginning and End.

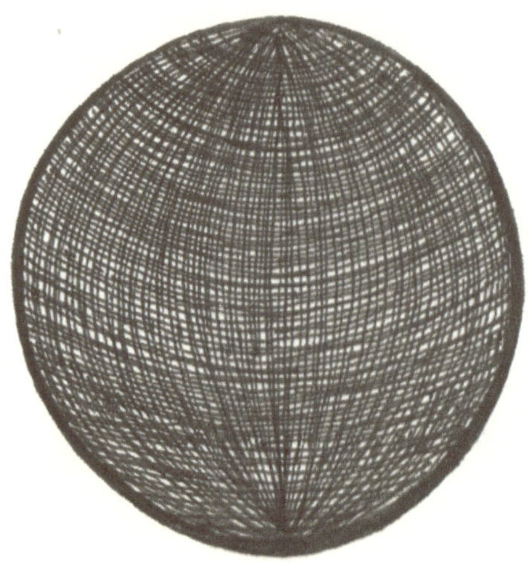

What does it mean to be Alpha and Omega?
What does it mean to be Beginning and End?
Where has He traveled that I've never traveled?
Where has He traveled that I've also been?
What does it mean to have always existed?
What does it mean to exist ever more?
Why does He call Himself the foundation?
How do we enter if He is the door?
How does He know what will be in the future?
Does it exist where my eyes cannot see?
Do I exist as I am at this moment
or is there, in fact, more of that which is me?
Does my life trace a path with its past, present, future
beyond three dimensions which I now perceive?
Is that what it means to view life through a mirror?
Is *to know there is more* what it means to believe?

There are no simple answers to
the greatest of all questions,
though man endeavors ever
to pontificate suggestions.
But Truth is so much greater
than the thoughts we can conceive,
that the greatest of debaters
cannot prove what he believes.

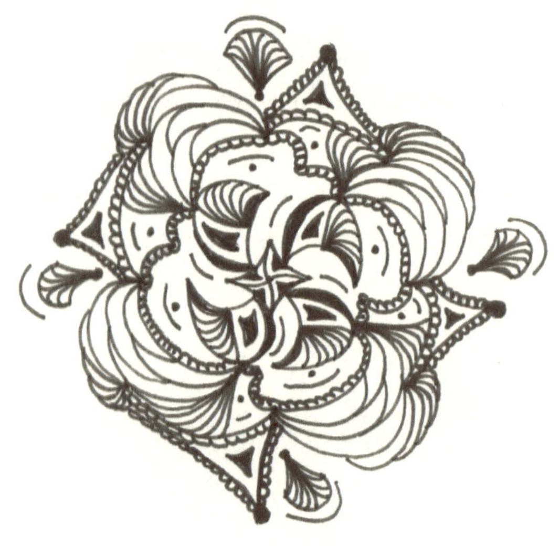

The rarest thing in all the earth is Truth!
In any form it's very hard to find.
It seldom lends itself to easy proof
and is not even easily defined.
To find Truth in a person whom one knows
is rarer yet – for most of us deceive.
It's not that we're not honest, noble souls!
We simply voice the falsehoods we believe!

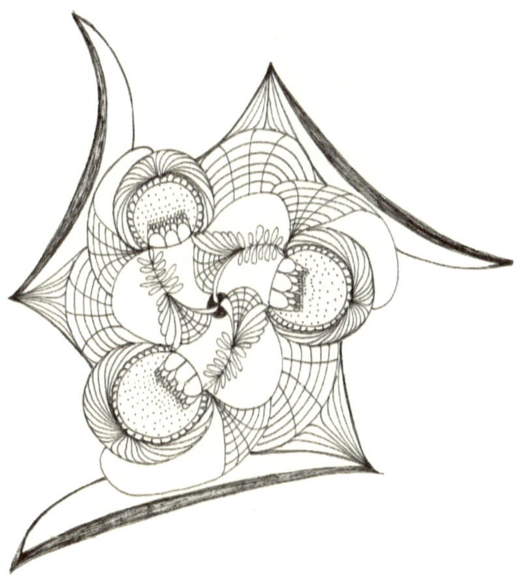

DIVINE BEING

I cannot comprehend immensity
like that of God eternal,
and, yet, I still must try!
Or else equate infinity with nothingness,
because my comprehension is so small.
But when I just begin to think
that all the vast expanse of heaven
may but form, like molecules,
a body, like a man's,
infinity belies the thought!
Eternity demands, that God, by definition,
also formed that great expanse!

The greater grows the universe,
the more I understand,
the more I comprehend the Thought,
I AM THAT WHICH I AM.

BABEL

Grasses nodding swiftly, caught in heated conversation,
fan the air and make the breezes blow –
while birds sing out in uncontrolled elation
and insects dance their messages below.
I sit and seek, but see yet no relation
between their gentle songs and words I know.
For God, who gave a language to each nation,
alone can hear the prayers that breezes blow –
while I, a child of mass communication,
in silence watch their conversations grow,
as grasses whisper secret information
and birds and insects simple truths do show.
Oh! Babel, your confusion's brought to bay!
Yet hear we half of what the world doth say!

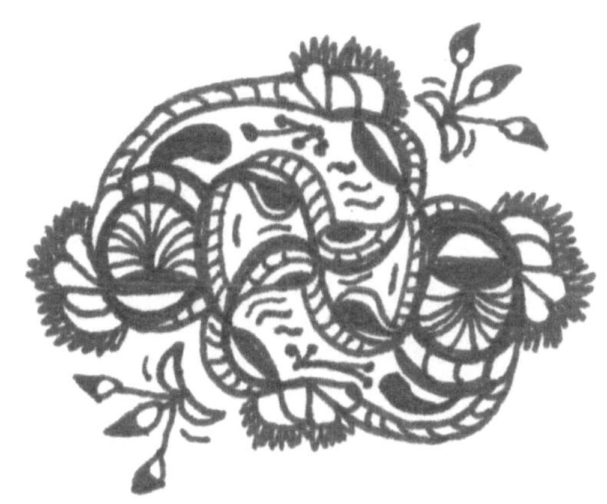

One of my daughters paints intriguing fairy tale images not related to well-known stories. The presence of dandelions growing in snow or of a woman with branches for wings invites each viewer to create a new story. *Calculated Chaos* is in some ways a mathematical fairytale inviting interpretation. Out of nothing but curved lines, the mind can create Chinese dragons ingesting black pearls, a series of destructive storms, dissonance extending to the ends of the earth, a ring of dancing chickens or four chipmunks with strange, bulging eyes. It is perhaps most satisfying, however, to put aside all need to define or make sense out of chaos and just savor the stillness of symmetry.

In our passion for making sense of a world in which orderly and chaotic elements are intertwined, our perceptions are so colored by personal experience and individual psychology that what we see often differs greatly from what the person beside us sees. We see the same individual lines, but not the same whole.

CALCULATED CHAOS is a hand-drawn conglomeration of lines with at-a-glance symmetry. The obvious algorithmic repetitions suggest order and direction, maybe even the idea that equations could be found to generate all of the curves, but unlike computer-generated forms where equations precede the images, this somewhat chaotic image is full of deviations from precision that make movement from image to equations a mind-boggling challenge.

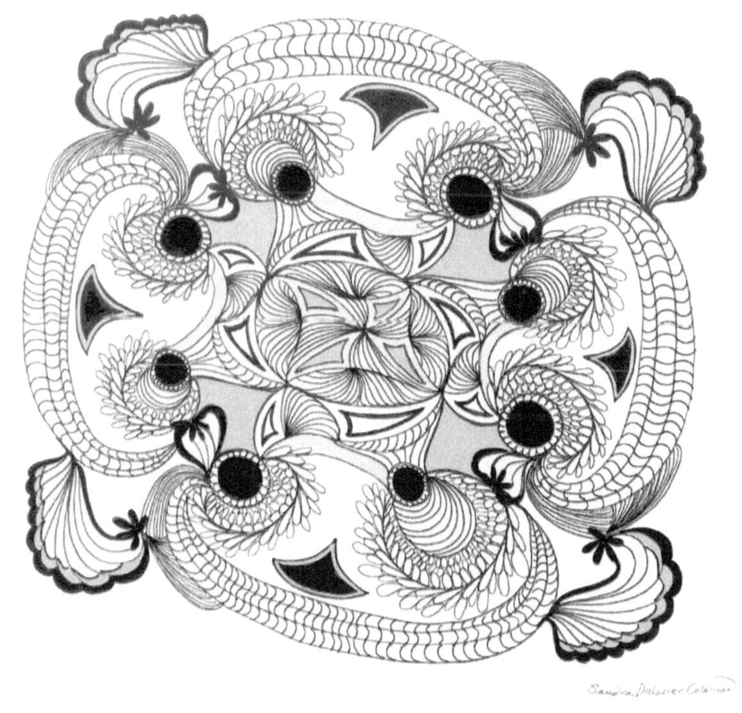

CALCULATED CHAOS
20" X 24"
Ink on Paper
2017

I see a world within a world –
a fractal fairyland –
where mountains, valleys, river beds
are sculpted in the sand.

On every mountain range I see
a smaller country still,
where smaller mountains, valleys, streams
converge upon the hills.

If I move closer – look again –
what wonder meets my eye,
as yet upon each tiny hill
another world I spy!

Had I a magnifying glass,
I wonder, would I see
another country lying there
still smaller than these three?

It's been said, in the Beginning,
there was chaos every place,
and that God spoke up and gave
a kind of order to our Space.
But, lately, we've discovered
that it's chaos that abounds,
and in every living thing,
it seems, some chaos can be found.
Still, it's such an ordered chaos
that it seems quite clear to me
that God creates with fractals
nature's true geometry!

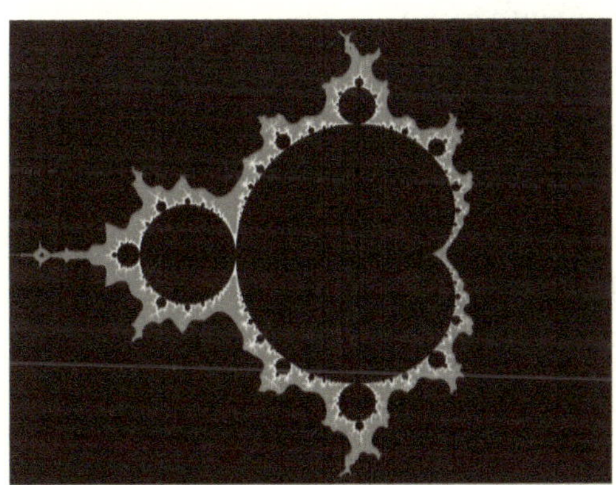

MANDELBROT SET

SMALL THINGS

I saw a black beetle
as small as a pin
crawl into a hole
and back out again.
So tiny and helpless
it seemed to my eye,
'til I realized that he
was the one who could fly!

I picked up a pine cone
that fell from a tree
and saw it was covered
with tiny brown seeds.
As I looked at the seeds
as they lay in my hand,
I saw life they would bring
where e'er they might land.

The next thing I knew
I was watching the sand —
the grains smaller still
than the seeds in my hand,
but though they were small
there was purpose in each,
for without grains of sand
there would not be a beach.

FIRST FLOWER

The details of a flower preserved in stone,
that bloomed some fifty million years ago –
provide one clue that serves to help us know
just how the first of flowers might have grown.
She seems to be a necessary flower,
essential to our having come to be,
precursor to the fruit of every bower,
to every grain on which we daily feed –
a flower – simple, scentless, but alive –
sufficient lure to pollinating bees,
not beautiful, but holding, yet, a power,
essential to its sexuality,
and, that, essential to all life we know
which on the fruit of flowers thrives and grows.

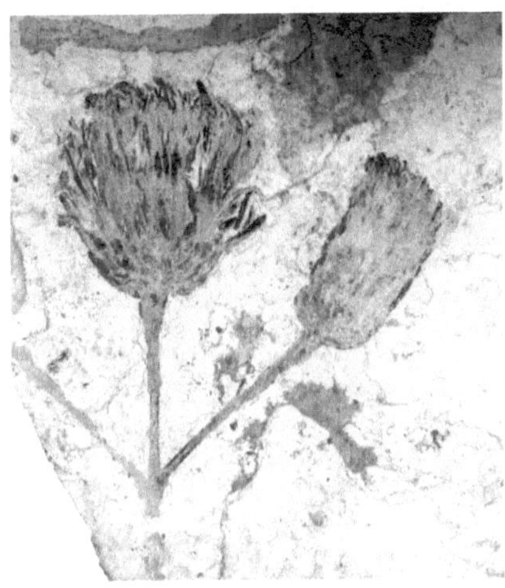

Some days just call for
touching
without talking.
On those days thoughts are
better left unsaid,
unless touching
simply cannot be
an option,
and then,
we try
to touch
with words,
instead.

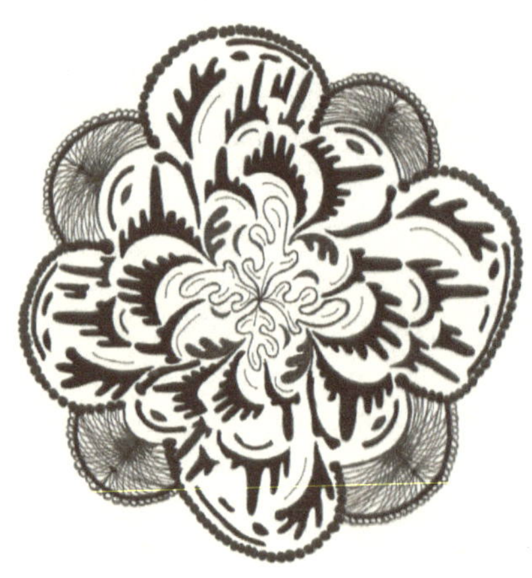

A hundred poems and still no words
to show what's in my mind.
To show my heart, I now am sure,
no words I'll ever find.
Words can't express the subtle thought
that eyes and touch express.
Words can't be borrowed, found, or bought
to rival one caress.

Touch me, hold me, gently like a bird –
warm and friendly alabaster curves –
red as leaves of autumn in the sun,
red as auburn tresses come undone.
Touch me, hold me, know me if you can!
See one opening? Better look again!
First there's one, then two, then none at all!
Don't give up until the mystery's solved.
Touch me, hold me, test my boundaries.
Could it be that there are two of me?
Polish, satin, gently intertwined?
Can mere touching satisfy the mind?
Is there more to me than meets the eye?
Can you know me? Dare you even try?

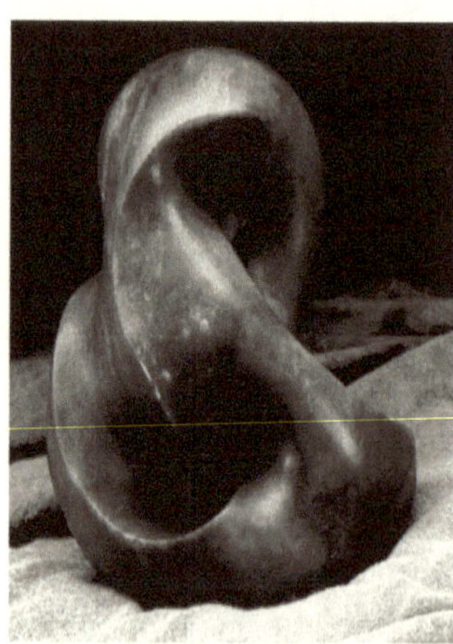

Figure Eight Knot Complement I
Helaman Ferguson, 1985
printed with his permission

INVITATION

A garden can be too neat and trim.
A pathway can be too straight.
It's better to let some plants begin
to cover the walls and gate.
A small bit of wildness is no sin,
for nature has things to state,
and flowers to whom free rein is given
will bloom and communicate.
When a garden where the flowers all blend
and even the trees aren't straight
invites you to come, to enter in,
there's no need to hesitate!

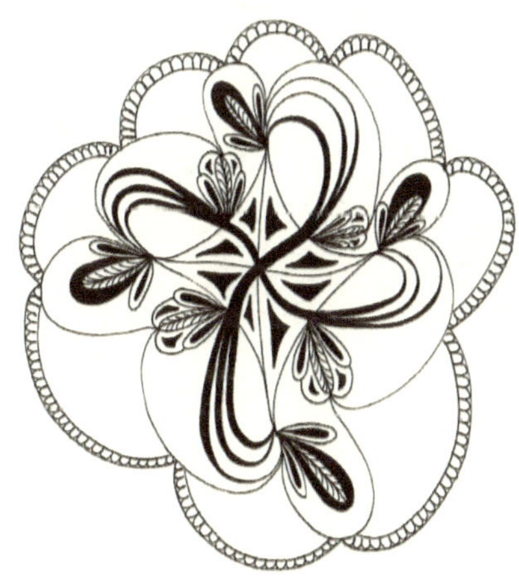

The wetlands are completely wild –
completely wild and free!
It seems so strange to stand inside
surveying all I see.
The outside wild – an untamed child
like what's inside of me.
The inside tame – all meek and mild
more like the me you see.

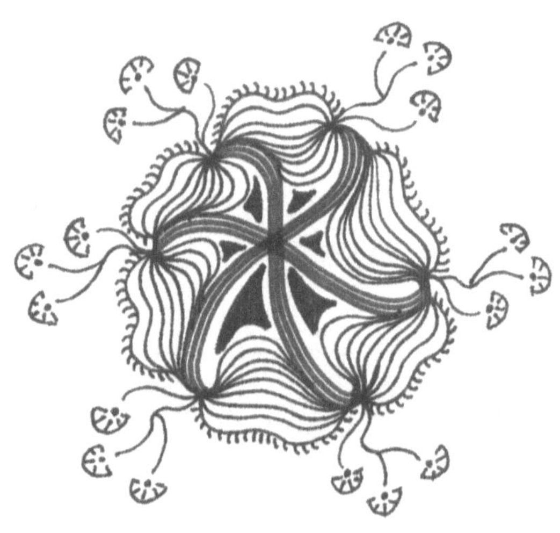

HUMMINGBIRD

A tiny hummingbird has learned to trust me
at least to trust I'll keep in good supply
the nectar, sweet, on which it daily feeds.
A hundred times a day it comes and drinks the
sugar water from the scarlet cup I
keep beside the window for his needs.
If I am cautious and I keep my distance,
sometimes he lets me watch him from inside –
but he would fly to safety in an instant,
if the door I ever dared to open wide.

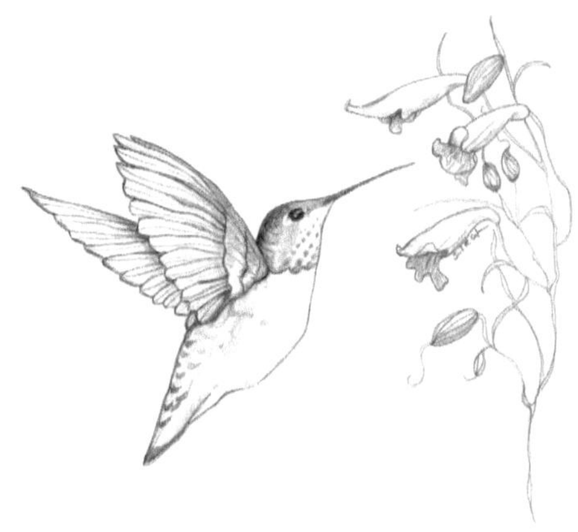

(ᴏɴ ᴛʜᴇ ᴘᴀᴛᴛᴇʀɴ ɪɴ M.C. ᴇsᴄʜᴇʀ ᴛᴇssᴇʟʟᴀᴛɪᴏɴs)

There is no way to draw a line,
other than a border line,
which splits what was a unity
into a multiplicity.
Whatever form the line may be –
pure orb or drawn haphazardly –
if closed, it forms, without a doubt,
two parts of space – inside and out.
All forms defined by borders are
perceived as either near or far.
That is, one form is viewed as space
on which the other form is placed –
unless the two-space world we build
is with congruent objects filled
in ways in which the whole defies
that one before the other lies –
or rather leads to thoughts more strange,
that near and far can be exchanged.
As endlessly the objects glide,
forming one another's sides,
we see within each entity
a fragment of infinity.

ꜰᴏʀ ꜰᴜʀᴛʜᴇʀ ᴇxᴘʟᴏʀᴀᴛɪᴏɴ ᴏꜰ ᴇsᴄʜᴇʀ's ʟɪᴢᴀʀᴅ ᴛᴇssᴇʟʟᴀᴛɪᴏɴ,
See https://www.geogebra.org/m/dQ6H3SsJ
http://www.seanmichaelragan.com/html/[2008-04-
18]_MC_Escher_lizard_vector_art.shtml

Banished from the perfect State
for weaving through emotion
what Plato deems a third-hand shade of Truth,
his student bids us "imitate"
with ardor and devotion,
declaring such catharsis has its use.
Through poiesis a soul can make
intoxicating potions
and dream realities defying proof,
where Truth and Falsehood sometimes mate
and Truth conceives new notions,
in magic realms where reason bears no fruit.

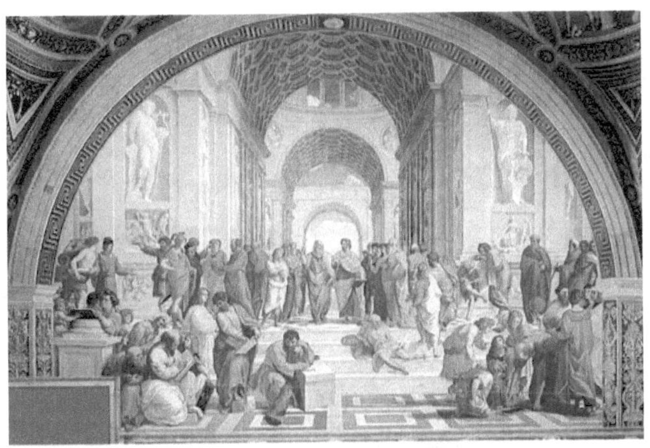

THE SCHOOL OF ATHENS
RAPHAEL (1483-1520)

Consider only what is real
and all of life's too small.
Complexity, though interesting,
may take no form at all.
But mapping complex to a real
can yield results surprising,
As singularities reveal
infinity arising.
Above the placid planar pool
an infinite tower reflected
is tangent by some abstract rule
and tangibly connected.

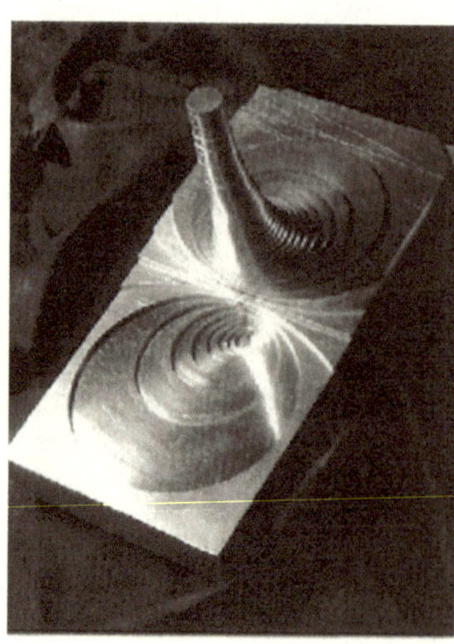

ESSENTIAL SINGULARITY
Helaman Ferguson, 1993
printed with his permission

Over, under, over, under
Under, over
Over, under, over, under
Serpent clover
Separate bases intertwining
with each other
Separate entities combining
much like lovers
Gently tangled, wound together
in a lover's knot forever
No beginning and no ending
from an earthly base ascending
in harmonic combination
Topological Creation

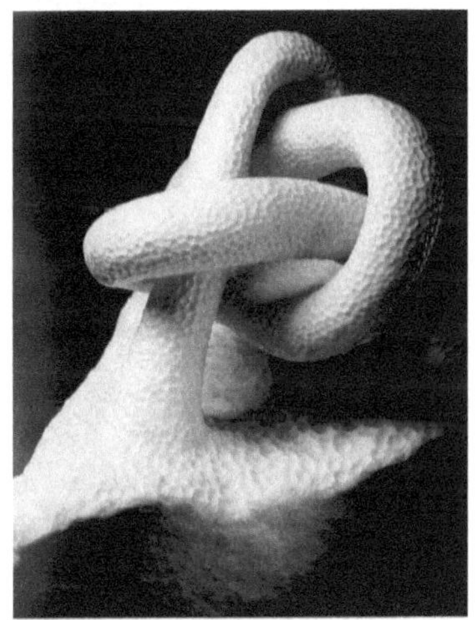

THURSTON'S HYPERBOLIC
KNOTTED WYES I
Helaman Ferguson, 1993
printed with his permission

Once there was a child of two
whom everyone agreed was you.
Then later on there was a youth
who, too, was you. Is not that truth?
At last, there was a full-grown man
you recognized as you again.
Now that you're older, more mature,
that you exist, you're almost sure!
And, yet, where are these other three?
They never died – where can they be?
Why don't we think it rather strange
to see our bodies clearly change,
while that which we would call ourselves
lives on inside of different shells?
To me, it's just as natural
to think of other lives as well,
and I am who I was before
much as I am the child of four.

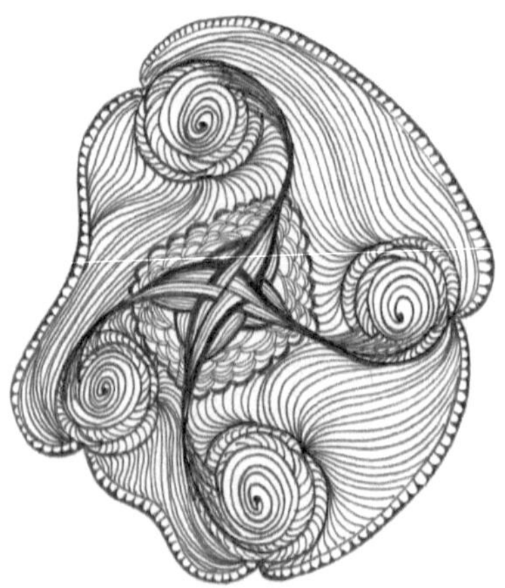

Not only has my body changed,
my soul has changed as well,
and which of all of these that were
is me, I cannot tell.
I've been the soul of innocence,
a soul mate, and a friend.
One who's loved with heart and soul,
but who loved in the end?
Am I the sum of all I've done,
or all my eyes have seen?
Am I my future, or my past,
or always in between?
Elusive though the moments are
that mold and shape my soul,
through all, I feel you loving me,
the fragments and the whole.

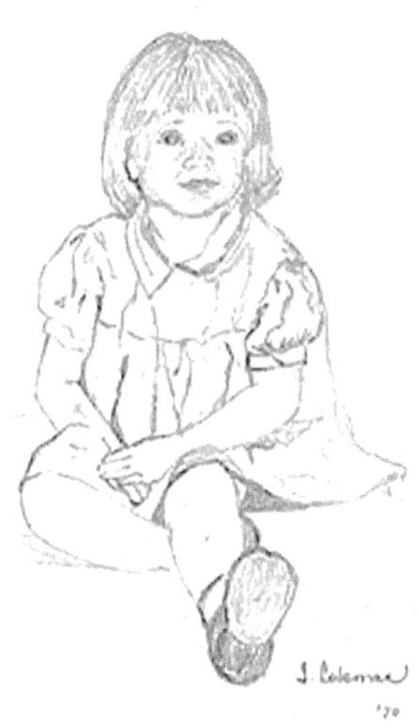

Ouroboros, serpent torus,
you yourself devour –
signifying earth and heaven
in each other's power.

Emblematic Ouroboros,
when at you I gaze,
I see more of light than darkness
in your scaly maze.

Ouroboros, crouched before us,
full of mystery –
in your complementary torus
inner you I see.

Avian torus, head just resting
underneath her wing –
counterpart of you, contrasting
each essential thing

even in her patterned surface
dark where you are light,
balanced even as the earth is
'twixt the day and night.

Perfect blend of space and matter
you would seem to be,
where in light and shadow gather
all eternity.

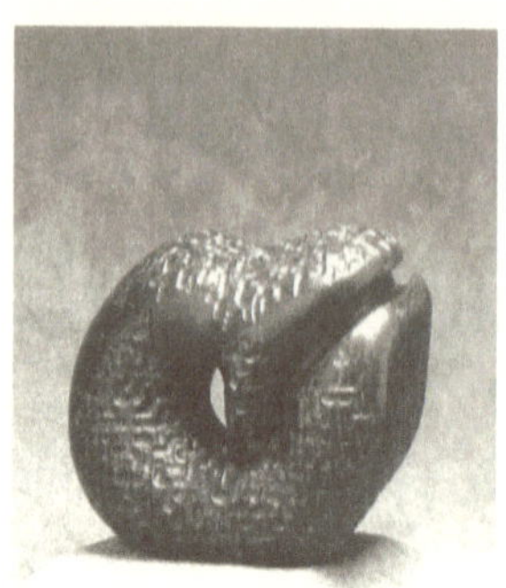

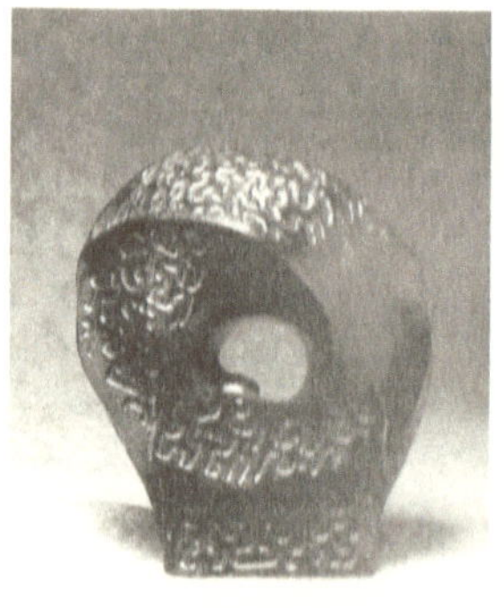

BIVARIATE CAUCHY KERNEL
Helaman Ferguson, 1986
printed with permission

UMBILIC TORUS SRC

SCIENTIFIC RESEARCH CENTER BECAME SARAH ROBIN COLEMAN
AFTER HELAMAN READ THIS POEM ABOUT MY DAUGHTER.

Beauty is no mystery,
but how it comes to be
eludes our grasp mysteriously
in physicality.
What is it in a certain curve
that makes it warm, inviting,
while yet another strikes a nerve
that conjures thoughts of fighting?
Mix beauty and vitality
and in the mating pair
springs forth a new reality
mysterious and rare –
both nurturing and threatening –
one form with shades of two –
a form demanding reckoning
from either point of view.

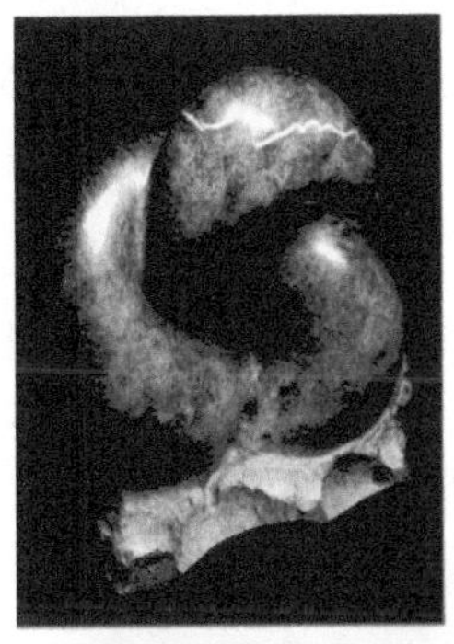

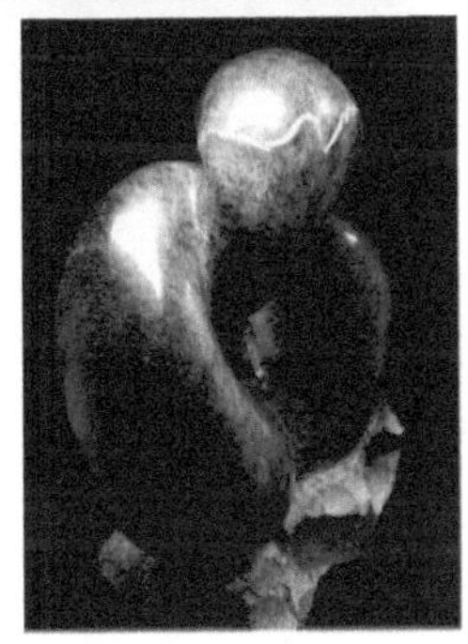

UMBILIC TORUS SRC
Helaman Ferguson, 1990
printed with his permission

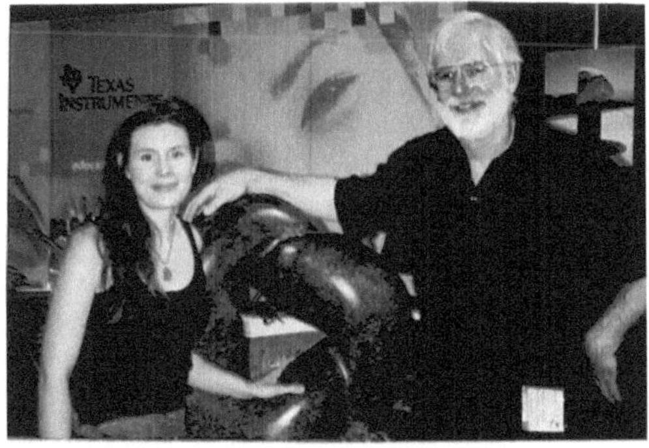

SARAH ROBIN COLEMAN AND HELAMAN FERGUSON

PERSPECTIVE

One point straight ahead in the distance.
You've seen all things as tending toward that.
What you've seen between you and the distance
has depended on just where you've sat.
The man who's been sitting beside you,
has been getting a different view.
Don't you see, what you see isn't certain,
since your view's so dependent on you?

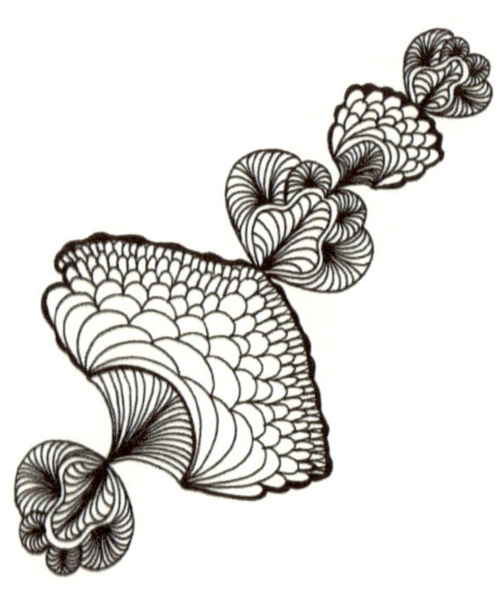

DALÍ'S HORSE

SALVADOR DALÍ HAD AN IDEA FOR AN IMPOSSIBLE SCULPTURE.
www.math.brown.edu/tbanchof/ups/group4/

From where I stand, the beast's a horse!
You must agree with me, of course!
I see his nostrils flaring wide,
behind his head on either side
his shoulders, muscular and strong.
It's all so clear! I can't be wrong!

I am deceived? What's that you say?
The rump's near seven leagues away?
And, viewing him from where you are,
the shoulders, too, are very far?
From what you say, it would seem clear
the horse I see will disappear,
if I allow the slightest move
from what I'm standing here to prove!

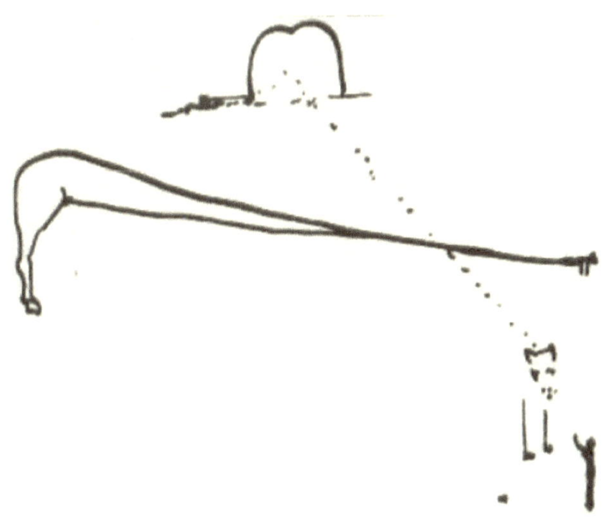

My interest in art with mathematical elements includes several forms of visual art as well as poetry. In my algorithmic drawings, I explore the effect of basing a hand-drawn design on a set of well-defined steps, where the steps become apparent through their patterned repetition.

In recent years, computer-generated images based on algorithmic repetitions have been the basis of a variety of interesting and beautiful works of art. Many of these images, such as those related to the Mandelbrot Set, are far too intricate and complex to be produced without the aid of a computer, although the generating algorithms are often quite simple.

By contrast, my pen and ink drawings are hand-drawn without the aid of technology or measuring devices. The designs generally employ a number of complex steps, which are defined just clearly enough in my mind to be repeated in an observable pattern. An interesting challenge might be to develop a computer program to generate near replicas of the hand-drawn designs.

Viewers often imagine in these abstract algorithmic designs some reflection of the natural world, although the designs are based on nothing existent in reality. The link to the natural world probably lies in the fact that most things that grow naturally grow algorithmically, moving through clearly-defined stages of development that result in interesting patterns and symmetries.

It would seem possible that a thorough mathematical analysis of an algorithmic drawing might create a bridge to a better understanding of the growth patterns of certain plant and animal forms in nature.

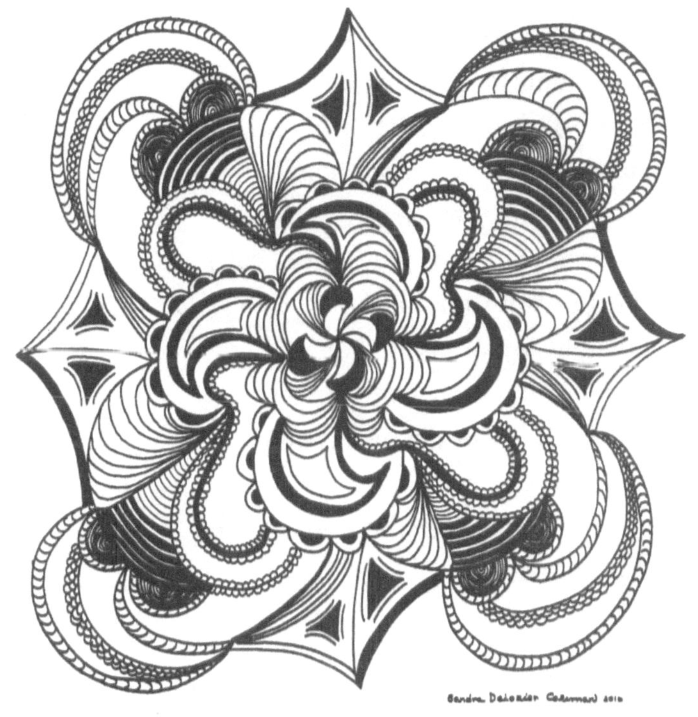

ALGORITHMIC PINWHEEL

25" x 21"
Ink on Paper
2010

One, two, three, four, five, six, seven!
Can we count our way to heaven?
Eight, nine, ten, eleven, twelve...
in what mystery do we delve?
Thirteen, fourteen, fifteen, then,
start to count by fives or tens.
Twenty, thirty, forty, fifty...
We're approaching much more quickly.
Sixty, seventy, take a leap –
Count by hundreds in your sleep!
First one hundred – jump to two!
We can count by thousands, too!
Even millions by the score
aren't enough. There's so much more!
Billions, trillions, zillions! Wow!
Are we getting closer, now?
Count up to a googolplex!
I can tell you what comes next!
It's a googolplex plus one –
Proof enough that we're not done!
Count as far as you are clever!
I can prove you'll finish, NEVER!

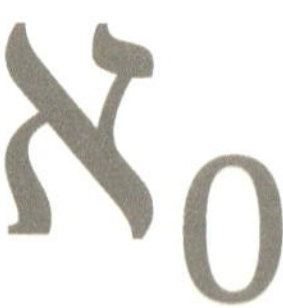

One gigantic set made of all that there is
boggles the mind with paradoxes.
For it's greater than all, but smaller than this –
the set which consists of the subsets of it.

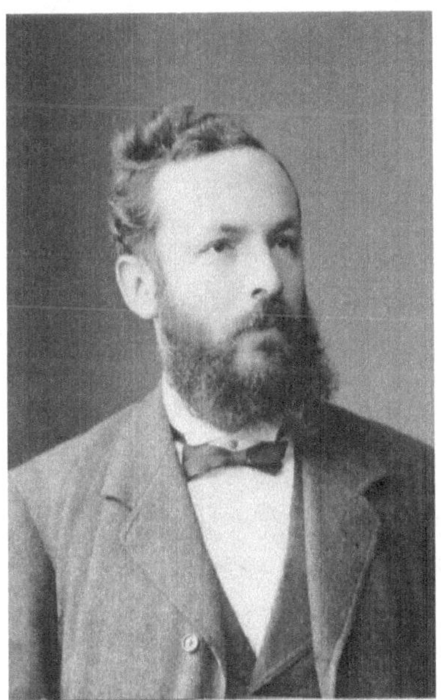

GEORG CANTOR (1845-1918)

S_1	=	0	0	0	0	0	0	0	0	0	⋯
S_2	=	1	1	1	1	1	1	1	1	1	⋯
S_3	=	0	1	0	1	0	1	0	1	0	⋯
S_4	=	1	0	1	0	1	0	1	0	1	⋯
S_5	=	1	1	0	1	0	1	1	0	1	⋯
S_6	=	0	0	1	1	0	1	1	0	1	⋯
S_7	=	1	0	0	0	1	0	0	0	1	⋯
S_8	=	0	0	1	1	0	0	1	1	0	⋯
S_9	=	1	1	0	0	1	1	0	0	1	⋯
⋮		⋮	⋮	⋮	⋮	⋮	⋮	⋮	⋮	⋮	⋱

S	=	1	0	1	1	1	0	1	0	0	⋯

CANTOR'S DIAGONAL PROOF

Though I can't write out all of pi,
the decimal does exist.
Yet, if I write until I die,
some digits will be missed.
Still, given any other Real,
it must be less, or greater,
and there's a way to order them,
if not quite soon, then later.
Give me as many as you find;
I'll place them in the list,
as long as they are well-defined.
On this I must insist!
I see you're doubtful of my scheme!
I'll never list them all,
for some are much too large it seems
and some are much too small!
Still others are so close to pi,
or close to one another,
It's quite a problem to decide
which comes before the other.
Yet, even so, you must agree
if we just keep expanding,
At last, it will be clear to see
with no misunderstanding.
It's true, the list is incomplete.
Quite true – but tell me why
you focus on the *one* left out,
while I'm still *listing* pi!

The list begins with zero
and ends with reaching one.
As for the numbers in between –
I'll show how they're begun.
It's easy to imagine,
a binary array,
which, though it can't complete them all,
still lists them in a way.
Half of them start with zero –
the other half with one.
I'm sure you've seen a binary tree.
You know how branching's done.
Each digit grows two branches –
a zero and a one.
This way of growing branches
goes on and on and on.
We may not make it to the end
before we're out of time,
but though we finish none at all,
no "missing one" you'll find!
The problem, now, of counting them,
though somewhat more involved,
may not be one which can't be done,
but merely one unsolved.
If we use aleph naught to mean
the first infinity,
I say the cardinal number
of our set is plain to see.

Two-to-the-aleph-naught's the count
of pathways we could find –
each pathway corresponding to
a number well-defined.
That this is more than aleph naught,
I grant may be the truth.
Still, I insist, to show that's true
requires a different proof!

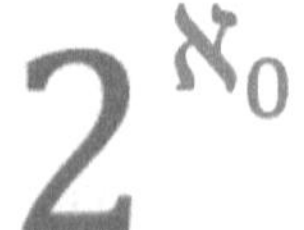

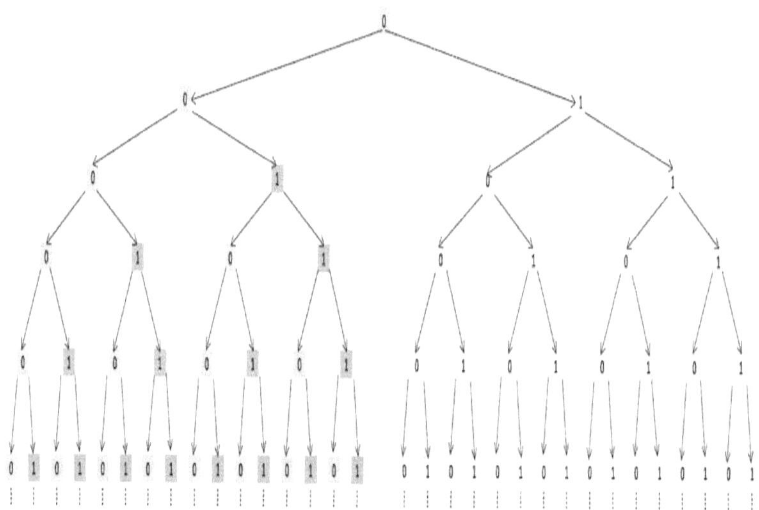

Can well-defined points ever build something real,
though infinite sets we define,
when we generate segments more empty than full
using points of the well-defined kind?
We fill up the gaps in between with such fluff –
names that go on forever, but how?
Since, to name even one, there is not time enough,
what can really exist here and now?
Do continuous numbers, in fact, change and grow,
and only exist as a whole
in the way living creatures are seen to exist
as their moments of being unfold?
There are only two true states of matter that matter –
in motion and frozen in time.
We can no more build something complete with the latter
than, with well-defined points, build a line.
The set of Real numbers consists of two kinds –
the continuous and the discreet.
Can we pair every one to some point on a line,
if so many are never complete?
Perhaps time is an integral part of the form
of everything real and abstract,
so that undefined numbers, like moments in time,
can in no useful way be exact.
Any object in motion determines a path –
though the pathway be ever so small –
where the number of points on the path is so vast
we have no way of counting them all.
Between two points that vary the least little bit,
lies a segment as dense as the line,
filled, perhaps, with expansions that only exist
in the context of motion and time.

A line is not composed of points,
though two a line define.
One cannot hope to build a plane
by piling line on line.
One cannot make of planes a cube,
because they have no depth.
Though piled to an infinitude,
the stack no higher gets.
It's harder, yet, to realize
the four-space hypercube,
though framed, indeed, by cubic sides,
is more than clustered cubes.
Each leap into a higher realm
requires infinity,
continuously out of reach
of single entities.

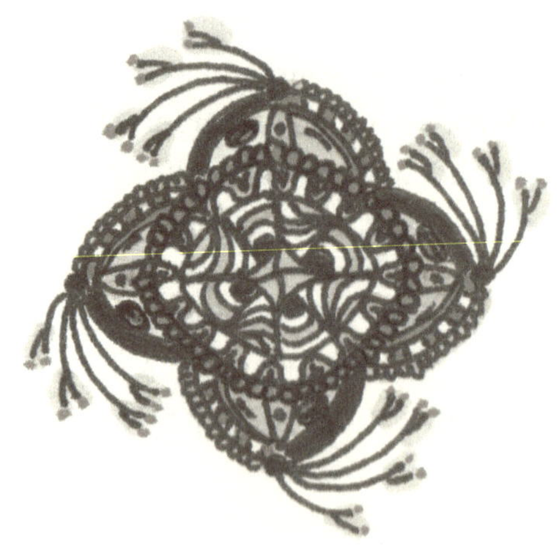

FOG

The strangest fog I saw today.
It hung above the ground
and seemed to take the world away
though sunlight did abound.

Where I was standing, all was clear.
Above the fog was light,
but everything beyond my sphere
was clearly out of sight.

Were this the normal state of things –
the view I saw today –
I'd have no notion anything
was there to take away.

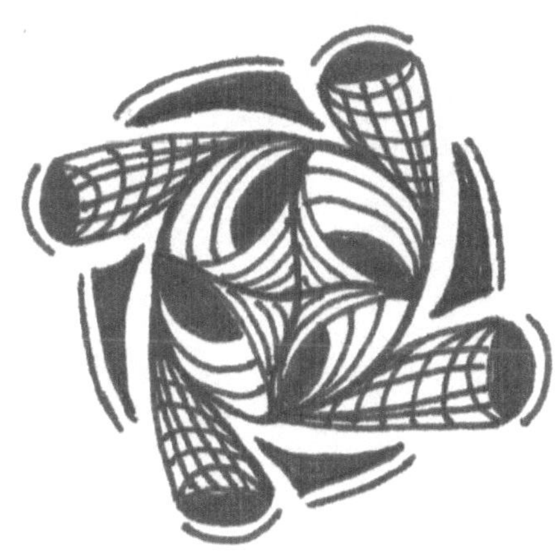

We cannot reach beyond the line
of what our eyes can see.
Thus, man's horizons must define
his own reality.
But, could not there be further out
realms bounded much like this,
where all we know beyond a doubt
is deemed not to exist?

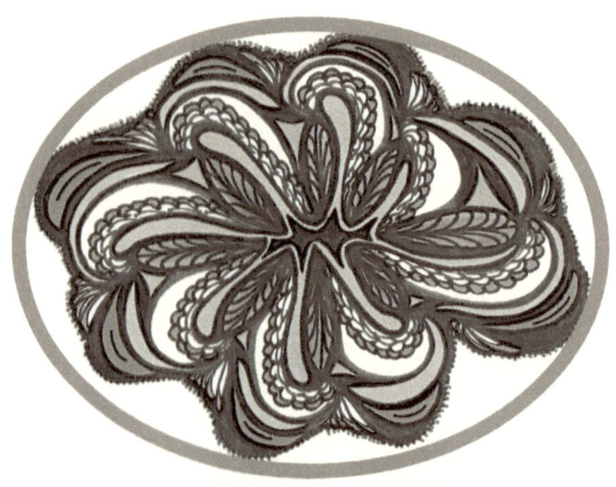

NONCONFORMIST

Everyone's a nonconformist
except for me.
All the people around me
dress exactly different
talk exactly different
think exactly different
and I'm the only one
who's still alike.

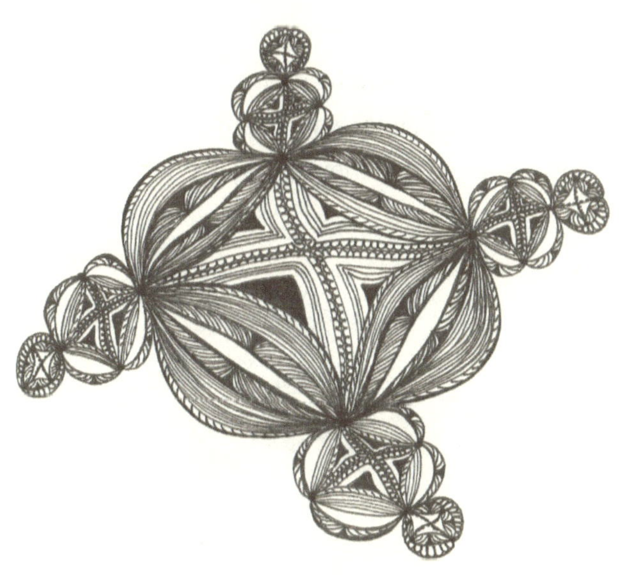

If we had had less digits –
just four fingers on each hand –
we'd think the way we count today
was hard to understand!

For then, it would seem natural
to keep count in groups of eight –
with ones and eights and sixty-fours
each falling in their place.

And if we tried to write a ten,
here's how it would be done!
We'd write 12, but really mean
one eight and two more ones!

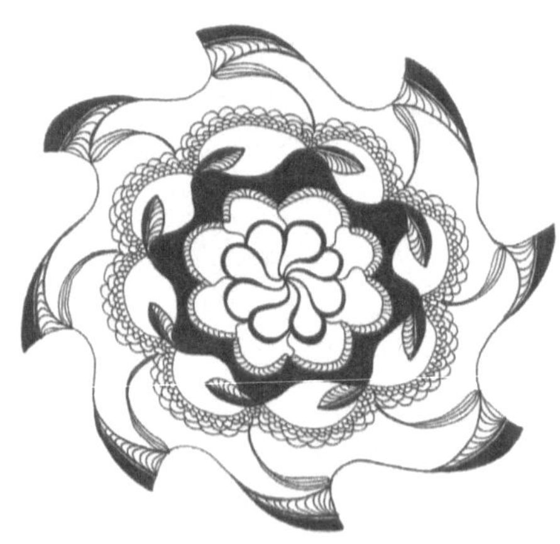

I can't believe there was a time
I relished games that teased the mind,
and found such puzzles very entertaining.
Today I opened up a book,
and gave the things a second look,
but this time only felt cerebral straining.
Who cares if Carter, Drake and Towns,
are barbers, architects or clowns!
No wonder all the students are complaining.
I really couldn't give a hoot
who plays the oboe, drum or flute,
nor shall I in the time I have remaining!
I'd rather travel, paint, or sing!
I'd rather do most anything,
than waste my time on something so constraining!

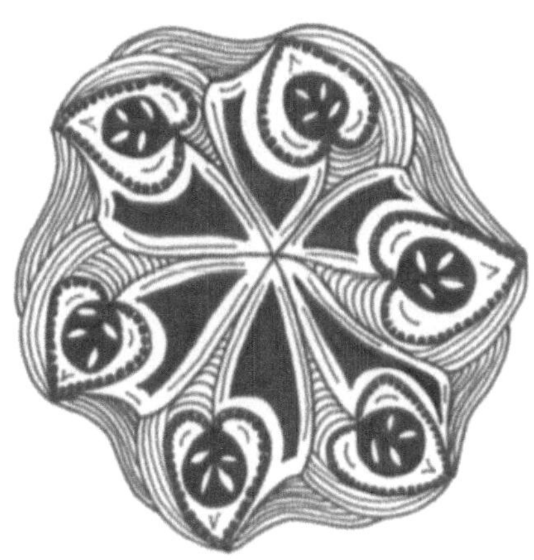

Returning from a Paris trip that allowed time for simple walks around our neighborhood, I have a renewed appreciation for a city built upon centuries-old, carefully-planned symmetries. Books have celebrated the doors of Paris, whose variously colored double panels are often ornamented with carved designs or surrounded by bas-relief sculptures, offering additional layers of symmetry. A favorite sight for visitors is a passageway in La Place des Vosges where a large arch for cars is flanked by two smaller arched passageways for pedestrians, all passing through and under a building that is a virtual tribute to symmetry. Rose windows, arched windows, symmetrical alcoves and columns fill so many churches and quintessentially Parisian buildings.

A compass rose can't begin to capture all that we saw, but creating this drawing in my usual style, without the aid of a computer or measuring devices, has allowed me to reflect on images that I found to be calming and beautiful because of the symmetries involved. This hand-drawn design, reminiscent of the old cartographers' aids to explorers, is my way of encouraging travel – especially quiet, unhurried travel. Not only in Paris, but wherever we go, if we take the time to look, we are likely to find that an affinity for the use of symmetry in art and architecture is both ancient and universal.

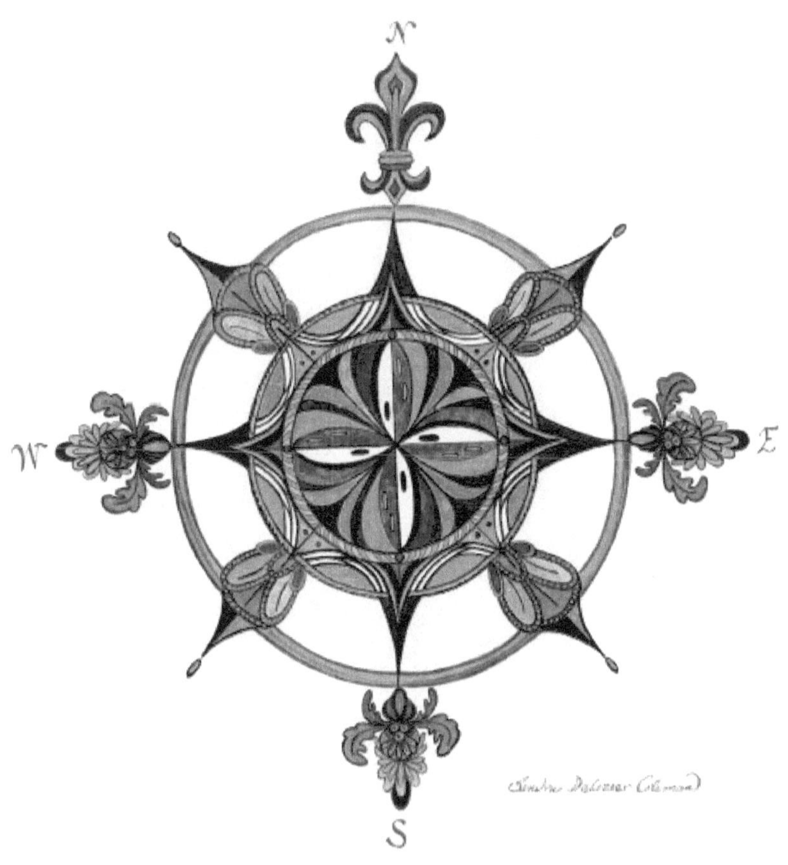

COMPASS ROSE
50 x 50 cm
Ink on Paper
2018

Everyone's the center of his own reality,
but some are suns that seek to shine on everything they see,
while others, pulling every light into their gravity,
like huge black holes, absorb all life in dark immensity.

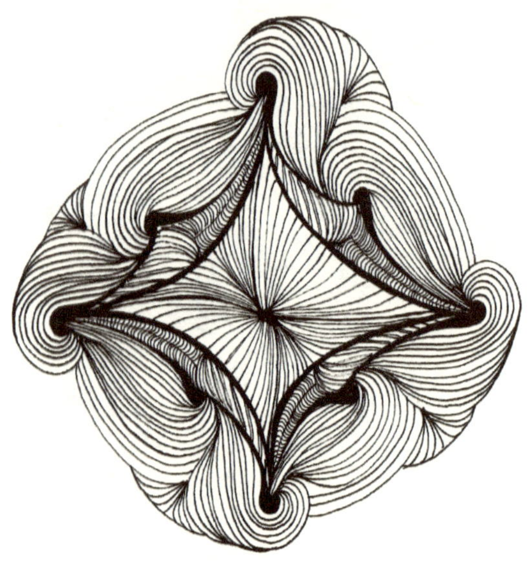

One Fuchsia Flower

One flower seems to think it's spring
though no one else agrees.
It's very busy blossoming
beneath the lifeless trees.
Its fragile, fuchsia petals
mid dry, brown leaves unfold,
oblivious to winter
and undaunted by the cold.

The mind can sometimes be a wall –
a barricade from harm –
and heart on head must sometimes call
when wakened in alarm.
One thought that helps a heavy heart
caught reeling in despair
is the thought that nothing can depart
which was not ever there!
Another trick the mind can play,
when called on to be smart,
is to reason – Friends don't go away!
and – Friends don't break your heart!
My head would have my heart forget
to keep from being blue!
But tricks aren't working for me yet –
I'm not as smart as you!

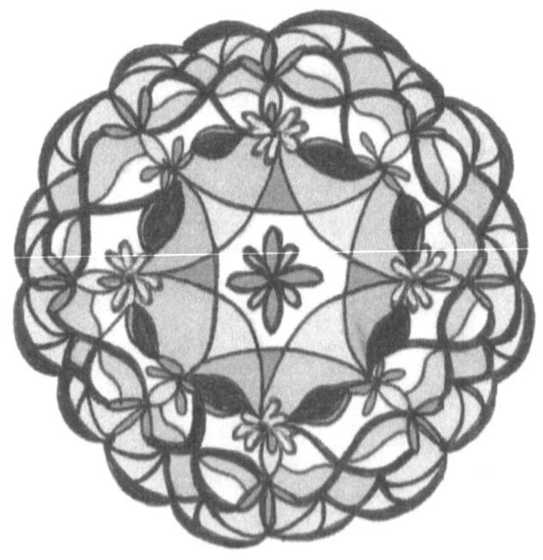

9(9+1)/2 Reasons to Be Happy

I saw a sunrise – only one,
but saw two bluebirds having fun,
three lovely dancing butterflies,
four seagulls in the clear blue skies,
five dolphins playing in the sea,
six green and white magnolia trees,
seven fishes jumping in the bay,
eight people sending smiles my way,
nine kinds of wild flowers in the wood –
all telling me that life is good!

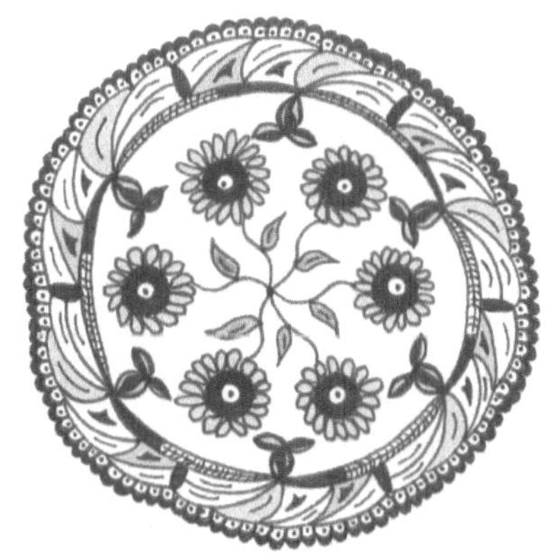

One problem I find
with having the mind
of both poet and mathematician
is that math-minded bards
often find it quite hard
to forgo a precise definition.
If they write about love,
they're in constant search of
what it means to be in that condition,
'til they reason away
what most poets would say
with a logically stated position.
The mathematical self
seems to reason so well
that those reading a poem wouldn't guess
it's been known from the start
love's a thing of the heart
mathematics can rarely express.

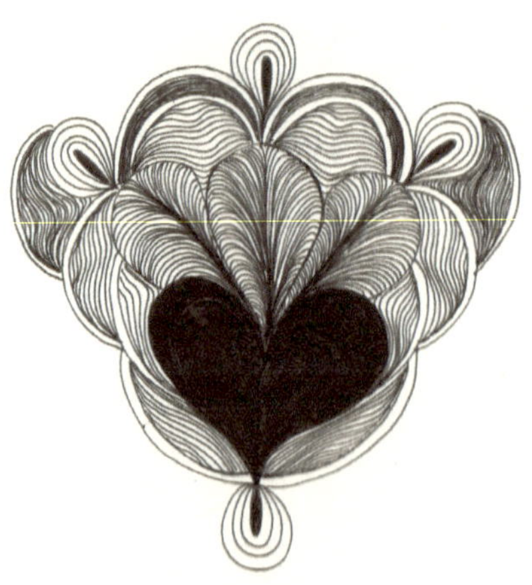

The proportion that's most sure to please –
(Any artist will say it's true!)
is when u is related to u + v
Exactly as v to u.

The emotion that's most sure to please –
(Just ask any woman! – Do!!)
is the feeling that tells her "You love me,
exactly as I love you!"

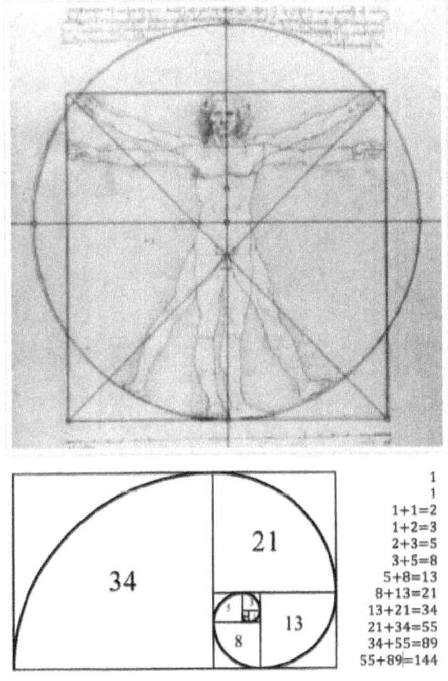

1,1,2,3,5,8,13,21,34,55,89,144...

You spoke to me of sculpture gardens,
wherein your forms of stone
would make your thoughts on mathematics
sensually known
and thrilled me with the passing thought
you'd seek to intertwine
among the images you wrought
a few uniquely mine!

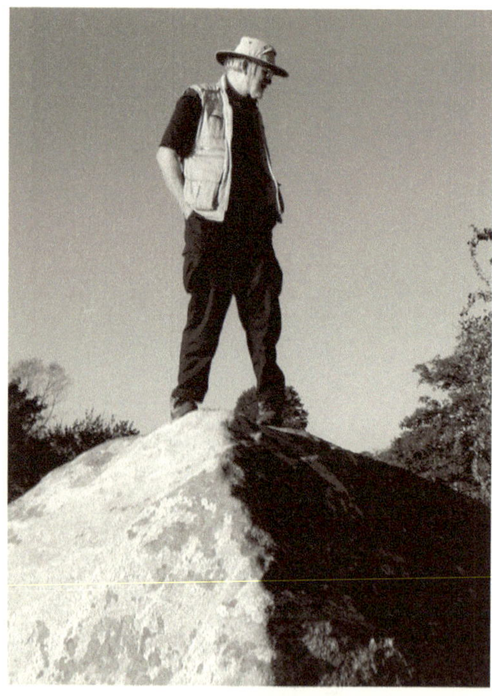

HELAMAN FERGUSON

THIS THOUGHT IN RHYME IS BASED ON A CONVERSATION WITH MATHEMATICIAN,
HELAMAN FERGUSON, WHO IS INTERESTED IN LINGUISTIC EVIDENCE OF PRE-
FIBONACCI AWARENESS OF PATTERN IN THE GOLDEN RECTANGLE.

On hearing of my thoughts on phi,
a mathematician asked if I
believed that Fibonacci's mind
was first in all the world to find
a pattern that is clearly there
when stones grow rectangles by squares.
He showed me how a calculus
could generate the sequence thus.

Beginning with a single stone
a group of rectangles is grown.
Add 1 x 1 then 2 x 2,
a special kind of shape ensues.
With 3 x 3 then 5 x 5,
each length to width grows nearer phi.

There's no real need to calculate
this wonder to appreciate,
for similarities are clear
as each new rectangle appears.

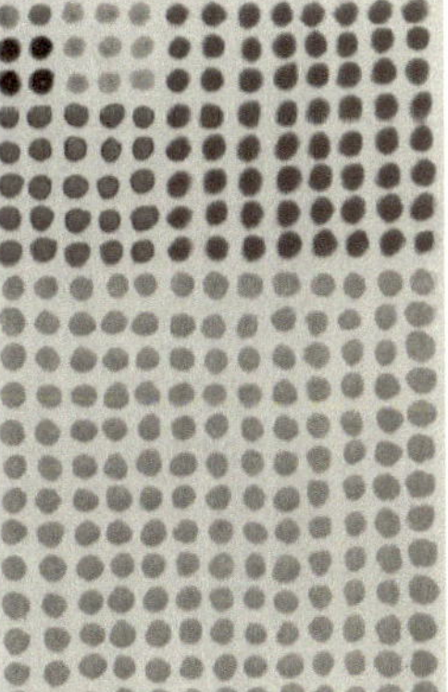

Thus, early man may well have seen
1, 1, 2, 3, 5, 8, 13...
as numbers having special traits
before he learned to calculate.
Indeed, my friend thinks this was known
since man began arranging stones.

An island in a sea of thought,
conjecture of abstraction,
arises 'til the mind is caught
and harrowed to distraction.
Was Goldbach wrong when he declared
that every even number
results from adding primes in pairs?
Or is it true? I wonder!
The sting has left Fermat's old thorn.
The chase has lost some spice.
But surely there must be a form
of proof that's more concise.
How many more elusive beasts
will rise up from the ocean
and challenge someone to defeat
a yet unproven notion?

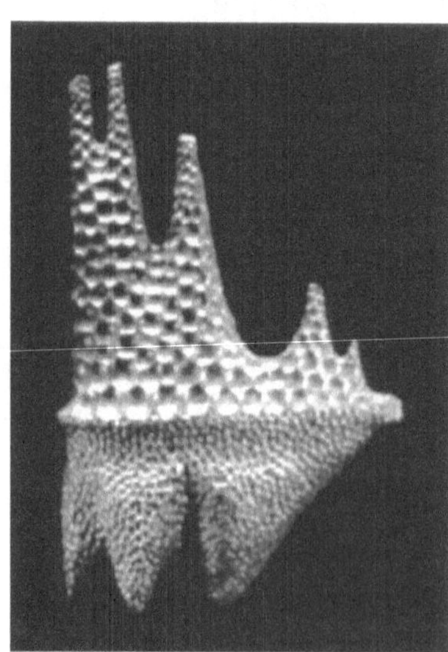

Igusa Conjecture
Helaman Ferguson, 1993
printed with his permission

"A little over five feet tall…"
Already you're like me!
Though not, perhaps, in your Carrara
perfect purity.
Still, somewhere in your strands that wind,
there's semblance of myself,
as I'm inclined to intertwine
what's me with someone else,
and give a little more of me
than one could well expect.
(I'd risk my life for love, you see.
I'm wild in that respect!)
And, yet, there are few openings
that penetrate my stone
(which might explain why, though I'm free,
I find myself alone).
I, too, reach ever higher,
though seldom reaching goals –
the end of all desire
being intertwining souls.

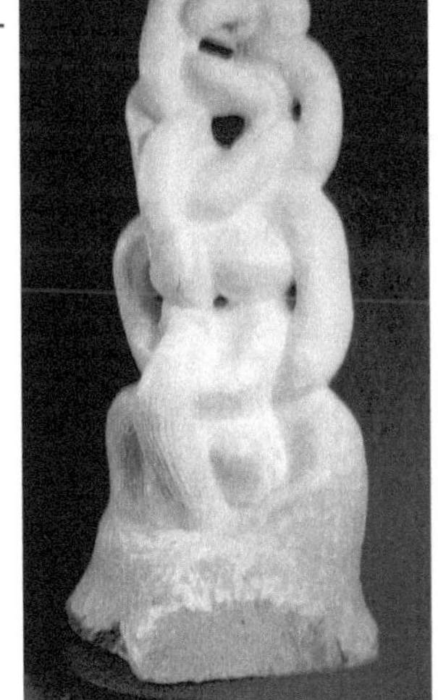

WILD SINGULAR TORUS
Helaman Ferguson, 1993
printed with his permission

I began writing poetry inspired by mathematics when I was an undergraduate student studying calculus. My interest in creating math-based art developed just a few years ago. My algorithmic designs are drawn freehand without the aid of measuring devices. Many are based on rotational symmetries where the first step is to estimate the location of points that divide the circle into equal parts. From there a design grows in the interplay of freedom and control – freedom to choose a succession of rules to follow, balanced with the need to follow each rule as many times as required for the particular symmetry to unfold.

Swirling Symmetry is an approximation of 45-degree rotational symmetry. There is an interplay of order and chaos in that rules have obviously been applied in an orderly way but with a sensitivity to initial conditions that leads to variations in scale within the eight repetitions. It is the choice to begin with estimations of compass points, rather than points determined by measuring devices, that creates interest, as the viewer analyzes, consciously or unconsciously, congruencies, similarities, and distortions in the orderly whole.

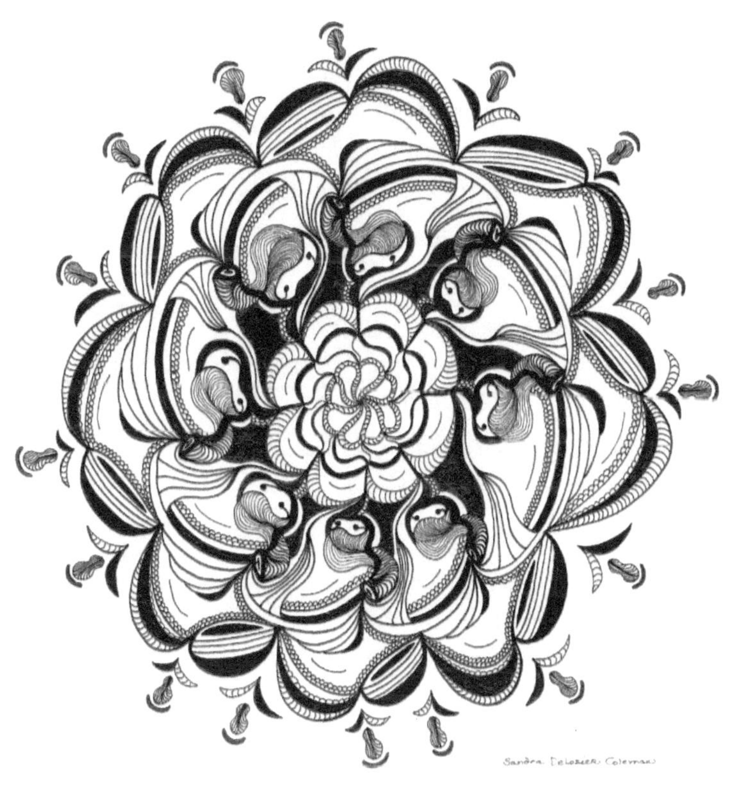

SWIRLING SYMMETRY
21" x 27"
Ink on Paper
2012

"Define a group," the student asks.
(I hope I'm equal to the task
of showing that by "group" is meant
more than a set of elements.)

We'll need a set that's well-defined,
where pairs of elements combined
are members of the set as well.
(He's with me, so far, I can tell.)

The rule for forming combinations
must hold for all associations –
although commutativity
is not a real necessity.

Except for the identity.
(But that's a special case you see!)

Indeed, this member of the set
is that peculiar element,
which paired with any other there
returns the other of the pair.

What's more, each member of the set
must have a partner element,
which pair combined must always be
this very same identity.

The student looks a little dazed.
Now, is he lost or just amazed?

That p→ q is true,
doesn't say very much about q.
For, if p should be false,
there's really no loss
in assuming that q could be, too.

On the other hand, q could be true.
So, what is a body to do?
With a false antecedent,
the consequent needn't
be something one lends credence to!

If the whole statement's false, then, my dear,
there is no ambiguity here!
For, then, p must be true –
but, then, not so for q.
I do hope that's all perfectly clear!

P	Q	$P \to Q$
T	T	T
T	F	F
F	T	T
F	F	T

Zero isn't "nothing."
If it were, there wouldn't be
a "whole" new set of numbers
when attached to 1, 2, 3...
and "1" would be the same as "10."
A googolplex, in fact,
would be no more than "1" or "10,"
if zero were like that!

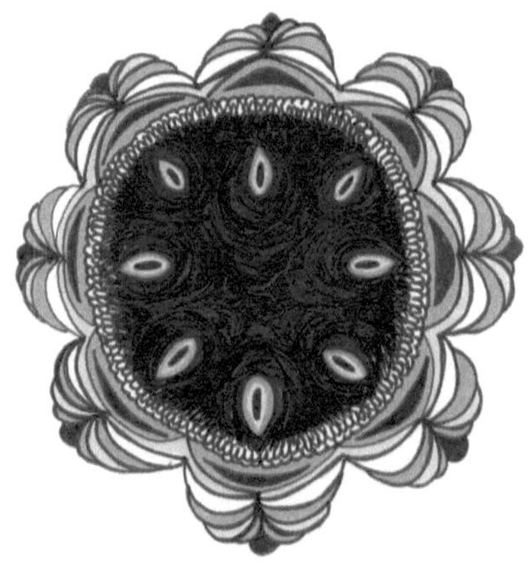

PROOF

When called upon, or forced, to prove
that zero's count is less than one,
define how "make less than" is done
by "Take a set and then remove
a little bit, a lot, or some."
This isn't hard! It might be fun!
You're catching on! You're in the groove!
Now, take a set whose count is one
and take one out. The proof is done!

Just when we all *know*
that these proofs are a laugh,
we're asked to *prove* zero
is less than one-half!

A few of us had really tried.
Some fewer, yet, had met success,
but only one – myself – had understood.
You stood before the class and sighed,
recalling how, when thus distressed,
you'd flung your book forever and for good!

You'd watched it fall from off the roof,
the pages flying everywhere,
like giant flakes of snow upon the lawn –
the end of problems, end of proofs,
the cage of nightly vigils where
you'd pondered theorems 'til the break of dawn.

You viewed your rage triumphantly
for something less than half a thought.
Then, found yourself regretting what you'd done.
So, racing to the clump of trees,
where, luckily, they had been caught,
you gathered up the pages one by one.

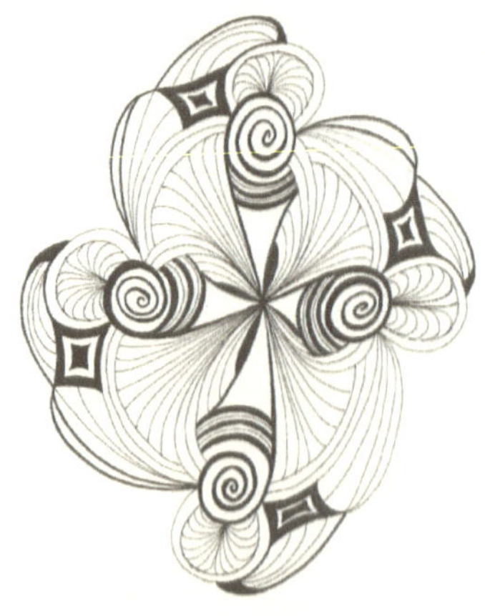

It's just as plain as plain can be
that 6 could be called 3 + 3.
And I'm as sure as I'm alive
that 8 could be called 3 + 5.
To get 10 or 12 – as sure as heaven –
we could add 3 or 5 to 7!
Do you begin to follow me
and call 14 11 + 3?
At 16 we would not be hurting,
for it's the sum of 3 and 13.
The pattern here that we both see,
I'd like to have named after me,
for I would bet my last thin dime
each even number's the sum of primes,
and that I could go on like this
for every one that you could list!
To prove that's true would take too long.
Let's see if you can prove me wrong –
or prove we'll never cross this hurdle.
Oh! Have you met my new friend, Gödel?

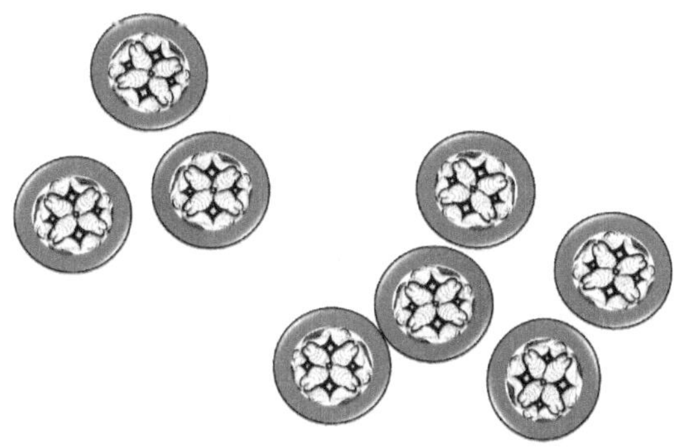

The moon was so full of himself last night
that he lingered awhile in the morning light
and spoke to the sun as she showed her face
in a coral gown, trimmed in golden lace.

"Begging your pardon," he said with a glow,
"but could we share the sky for an hour or so?
The night seemed so short, and I'm feeling so fine.
Would you mind very much if we both were to shine?
I'll keep to the west, and with you in the east,
I won't interfere with your show in the least."

The sun, always gracious, warm, loving and kind,
replied, "Be my guest, for I really don't mind.
In fact, I'm quite happy to see how you glow.
It's like seeing myself in a mirror, you know."

The sun from far away attracts the ocean,
but distance is itself a mighty force.
The moon, the smaller orb, by being closer,
affects his moods and actions more, of course.
The moon, it seems, controls his daily motion.
He comes and goes, a slave to her desire.
Yet, somewhere deep within the mighty ocean,
the sunlight feeds warm currents with her fire.

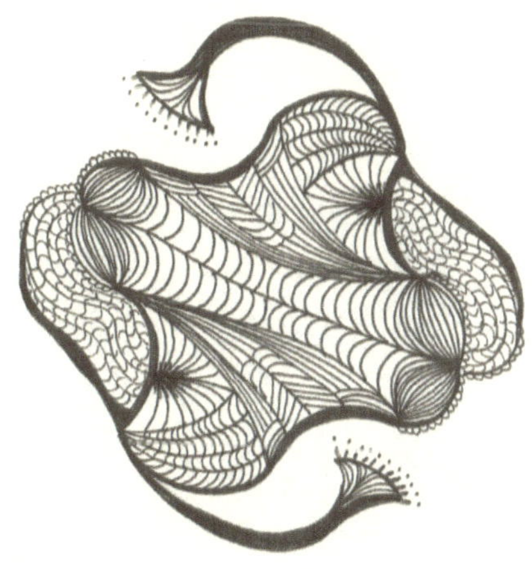

It's not easy to tell from the surface
what the ocean is holding inside.
Is the mystery there for a purpose –
life obscured by its surface so wide?
On the sand life's so very apparent,
though, there, too, lives much more than we spy.
Still, it's strange how the water transparent
hides its store 'neath a veil of the sky.

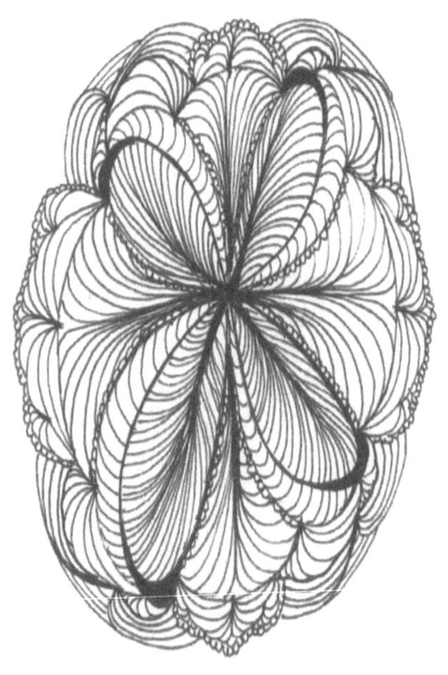

How must it feel to be the sea
and hold such life within,
hidden beneath the surface every day,
while fishermen sailing with the breeze
throw nets and taut lines in,
hoping to take some hard-won prize away?
How calm and tranquil – how like glass –
your surface blue can seem,
while life abundant thrives en masse
and multiplies unseen.
I'm not content to sail on high,
accepting a sportsman's part.
I'd rather be a mermaid, aye,
and swim into your heart.

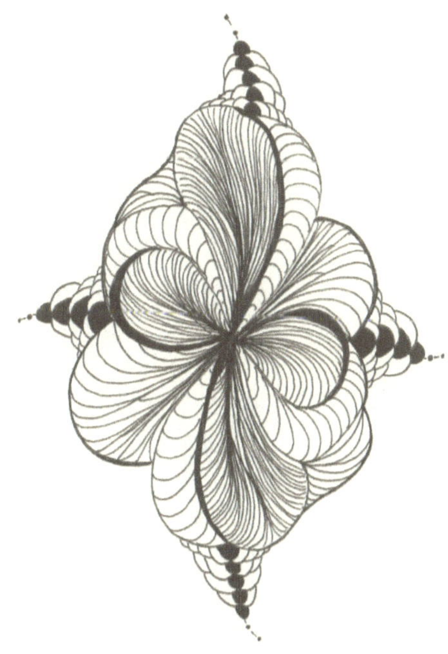

COMFORTER

Innocent you might say we were as doves –
each harboring a certain kind of love.
We three alone together in the basement –
she folding laundry there in the adjacent
room, as we sat silent, watching from a sofa by the wall
something mathematical – not inspiring us at all.
You were so stiff in your sincere desire
to be so innocent and so devoid of fire –
so careful not to let your body touch
the body of the soul you love so much.
Seeing from the washroom where she was
how cool we were – how cool the basement air –
she brought a comforter and spread it over us.
It seemed to me, I heard her whisper, "There!"
As though she gave permission, in her way,
for us to be less distant on that day.

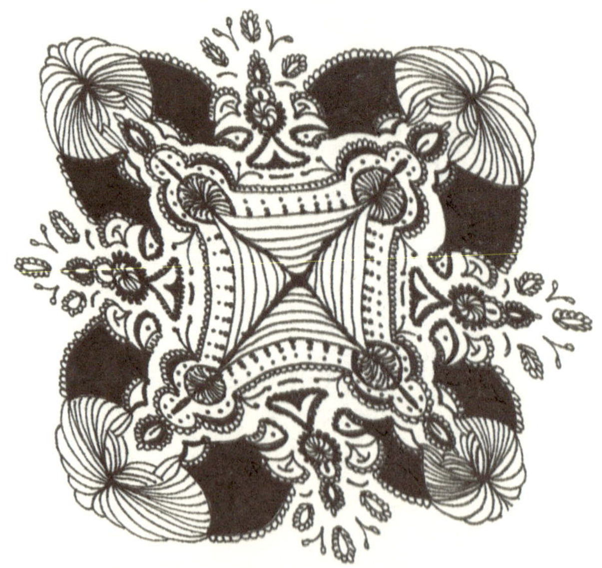

Don't look for me this evening!
It will be a useless search!
For, I'm occupied with reasoning,
and I'm lost in my research!
Don't tell me you're asthmatic –
you can't catch a breath of air!
I'm so lost in mathematics,
that, today, I just won't care!
Don't read me any poems today!
No thoughts on Love or Truth!
Oh! Won't you, please, just go away?
I'm working on a proof!

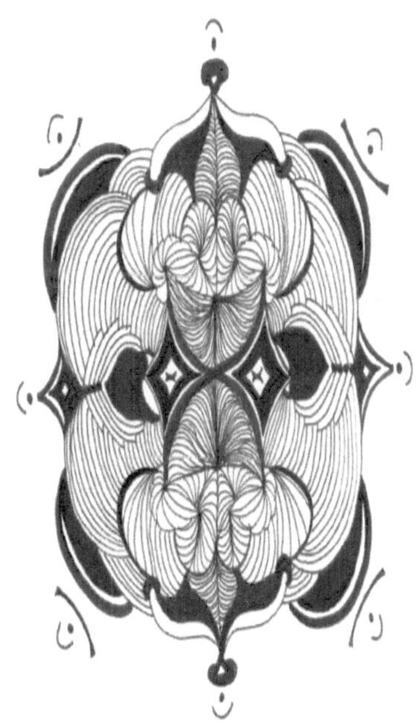

I can't remember how it felt
to lose myself in number,
in logic, proofs, and reasoning.
I simply can't remember!
Nor can I feel the way I felt
when love was all that mattered.
My mind and heart feel torn, abused,
neglected, lost, and scattered.

I have less chance of knowing you
than of writing out the root of two.
How e'er I start, it never ends,
exploring how love lies, pretends.

At least, as this square root unfolds,
the mind accepts what it is told.
The root of two is less than two,
but more than one, it's clearly true.

And it is easy to derive
that it is less than one point five.
It's just as easy, what is more,
to see it's more than one point four.

Just form the squares of these two stems!
Two lies between the two of them.

Thus, we may show it's greater than
a one point four one four two one
and that it's surely lesser, too,
than one point four one four two two.

But with such fine precision gained,
I find my interest has waned,
and back I go to figure out
your truths entwined with threads of doubt.

$$\sqrt{2} = 1.41421356237\ldots\ldots\ldots\ldots\ldots\ldots$$

I ask you, please,
if no one sees,
does anything appear?
And would you say
words thoughts convey
if no one's there to hear?
Now, what's the use
of seeking proofs
that no one will go near?
What use, my friend,
to frame my thoughts
in paintings, proofs, or words,
if in the end
my work's not sought,
seen, thought about, or heard?
It's really getting harder,
getting harder all the time,
when there's no satisfaction
or reward of any kind,
to find a reason or a way
to occupy my mind.

How oddly I myself divide
between the cipherer and the scribe!
Not quite a mathematician – no,
and whether poet, you would know!
Ten thousand problems I uncoiled
cannot redeem the hours I toiled,
reworking what brought others fame,
without one thought to gain a name.
So long, it was my pure delight
to stretch my mind both day and night,
unraveling syllogistically,
symbolic number's mysteries.
Until, one day, I know not why,
my passionate love for numbers died,
as though my mind became aware,
I'd find no satisfaction there.
Another passion came to be
the object of my destiny,
and I began to write my thoughts,
(which effort, too, may come to naught!)
Still, I am lured to put in rhyme
the things I feel from time to time,
and, now and then, flow from my hand
poems mathematicians understand.
A strange ménage à trois occurs
for me, my numbers, and my verse.

"Write back to her? Well, what's the point?
I don't see why I should.
She's written a few papers, but
I doubt that they were good.
I know that she's not famous.
What could she do for me?
She's certainly no beauty.
Why, she's almost seventy!
I'll bet she has a crackly voice
and nothing much to say
and I have more important things
I need to do today.
It's true she praised my paper
like no stranger's done before,
and that did make me happy
and inspired me to do more.
But write to her and tell her so?
I just don't feel inclined.
Today I have a lot less love
than research on my mind."

As troubling and as puzzling
as your thinking tends to be,
at least your unresponsiveness
is not reserved for me.
Unstinting praise you disrespect
and speak of with disdain,
regardless that the side-effect
could be another's pain.

ARCHIMEDES' END

Archimedes praised the lever
for all that it was worth –
declaring, with one long enough,
a man could move the earth!
He counted grains of sand required
to fill the universe
and said we'd need precisely
10^{23}.
Discovering in the bath one day
why things float and don't sink down,
they say, in haste to spread the news,
he ran naked through the town!
To understand the circle
was his passion 'til he died.
He even found a useful way
of generating pi.
One day a soldier saw him
drawing circles with a stick.
He spoke to him and seemed to think
his answer should be quick!
But Archimedes' mind
was in his math thoughts so absorbed,
he scarcely heard the soldier speak.
His comment was ignored.
The soldier, feeling angry
at the poor response he got,
pulled out a sword and killed
poor Archimedes on the spot.
Ye! Mathematicians! Learn from this,
that though your thoughts be deep,
sometimes it's best, when spoken to,
to take the time to speak!

ON WEIERSTRASS' OBSERVATION

You've never really understood my working problems,
whole books of them that have been solved before –
while I wonder how you read so many poems
without longing for the chance to write one more.

Someday, you'll write a poem so warm and tender,
the world will wonder where you found such truth,
and I'll contribute something they'll remember –
a long-sought-after, complicated proof!

Do you think that they were lovers?
he asked me.
I thought about it –
Thought of all the books that I had read –
Thought of all the things that had been said.
I think that they were closer,
I answered.
Close enough to talk about it, yes.
Too close to risk their love for that, I'd guess.

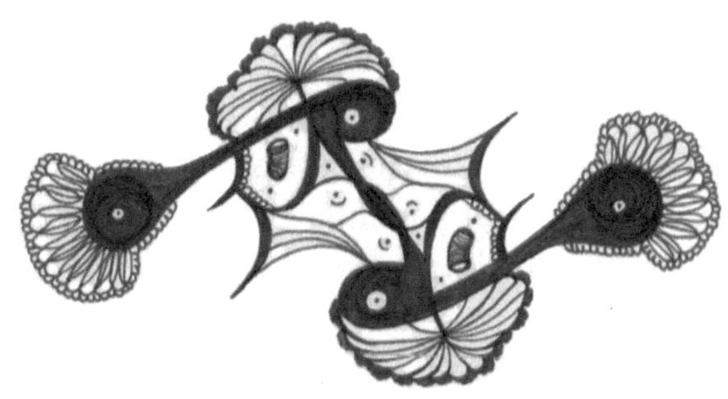

Sofia Vasilievna Kovalevskaya earned a PhD in mathematics at a time when women were not even allowed to attend classes. She eventually obtained a faculty position, went on to win the Prix Bordin, an honor as great as winning the Nobel Prize, and served as editor of the mathematics journal Acta Mathematica.

In addition to her achievements in mathematics, Kovalevskaya was recognized for her writing. She published a much-acclaimed autobiography, A Russian Childhood, a novella, Nihilist Girl, and two parallel dramas, How It Was and How It Might Have Been.

She explained in a prologue to the dramas that she intended to illustrate the idea that extreme sensitivity to initial conditions, as demonstrated by Poincaré in his research on the three-body problem, may be involved in the way very small differences in personality traits change the courses of people's lives by influencing choices made at critical moments.

In each of the plays, six young people's lives are romantically intertwined. The six nearly-identical characters in the two plays vary only slightly from the first play to the next. The slight dissimilarities in their natures are never-the-less sufficient to lead them to make significantly different choices at critical moments, leading to very different endings.

This illustrative drawing, like the plot, unfolds from the fires of an Ivan Kupala's Eve celebration. From there, a 60° rotational symmetry pattern represents both sets of six characters, who are understood to have traveled parallel paths until a crisis leads to radically different responses. The resultant opposite endings appear as two contrasting, overlapping 120° symmetries, where the shapes of the outer curves reflect a change in how the characters' lives have been paired.

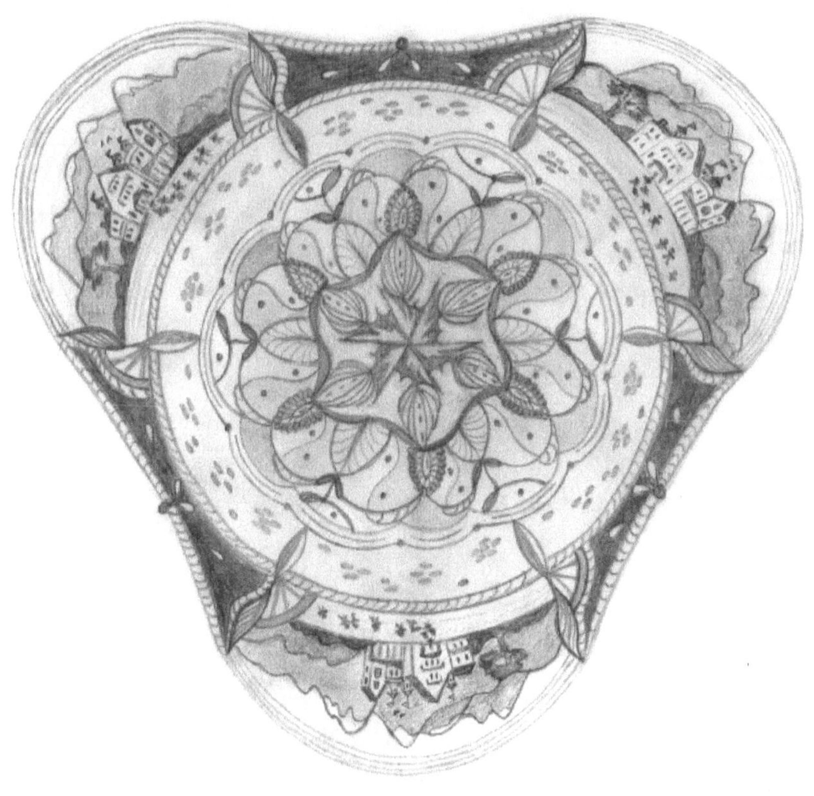

HOW IT WAS AND HOW IT MIGHT HAVE BEEN
28 x 28 CM
Graphite on Paper
2021

Poems and plays of Sofia Kovalevskaya appear in the book
MATHEMATICIAN WITH THE SOUL OF A POET
by Sandra DeLozier Coleman

Chaotic Thought

If a butterfly with a flap of its wings
halfway 'round the world
can cause such devastating things
as raging winds unfurled,
why should it seem so strange to me
that three or four words spoken
were misconstrued to such degree
that both our hearts were broken.

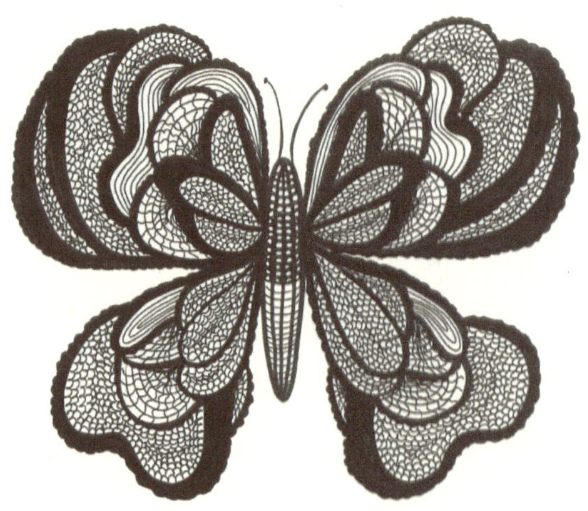

How have we changed the world ahead –
foregoing love to hate, instead –
when tiniest motions we observe
eternally alter the universe?

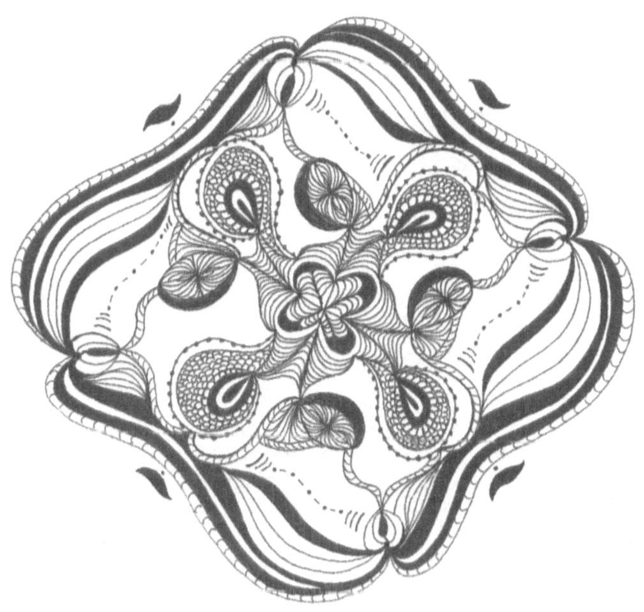

A tiny choice I made today
affects your world and mine.
How much is changed and in what way
must manifest in time.

Had I selected differently,
to branch in different ways,
what might have been that will not be
I cannot truly say.

I only know I made this choice
the way I make them all,
believing, in this universe,
great change begins with small.

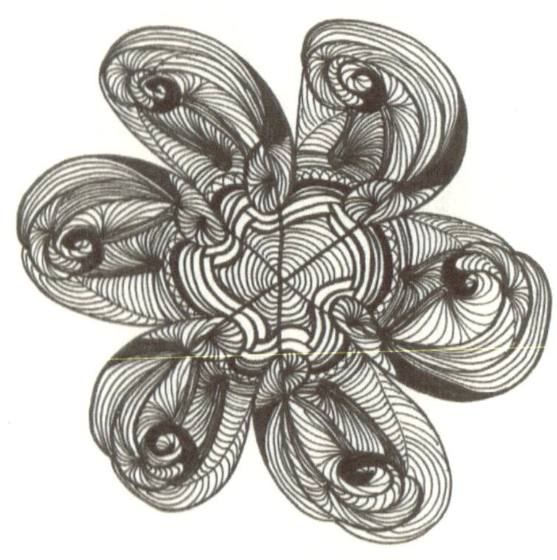

If and only if you love me
will I offer love to you.
If and only if you need me
will I say I need you, too.
If and only if you want me
will I want what lovers do.
Jove, in love, finds lies amusing.
Does he laugh at lover's truths?

P	Q	$P \leftrightarrow Q$
T	T	T
T	F	F
F	T	F
F	F	T

Who would not watch a sculptor's hands
intently, should she have the chance,
observing every turn and twist,
the movements of his fingers, wrists,
to see an object taking form,
a thought, as matter, being born?
Who would not want to hold, possess,
an artist's feelings, thus expressed?

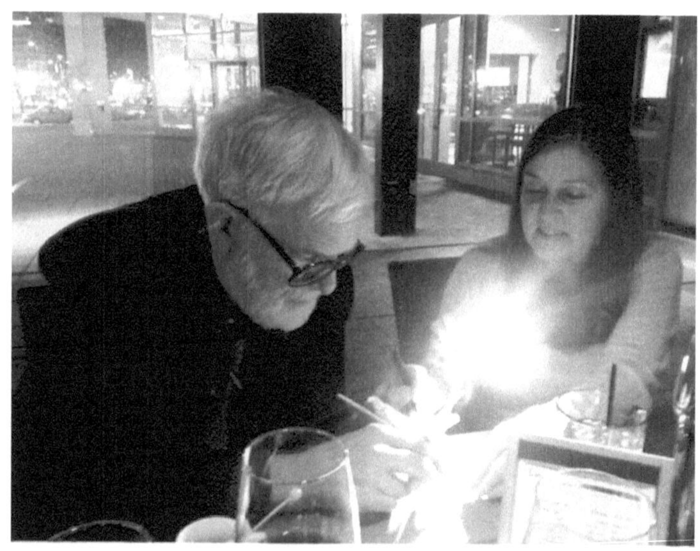

HELAMAN FERGUSON AND SANDRA DELOZIER COLEMAN

ENTANGLEMENT

Connected in some unseen way,
entangled though apart,
alike in physicality
and matters of the heart.
If any should be well or ill,
despondent or elated,
the others' being up or down
is cosmically related.
As GHZ tried to explain,
it seems it may be true
that when one particle is changed
another changes, too –
too quickly to be called effect,
too clearly to be chance,
entangled pairs of particles
perform a cosmic dance.
Entangled groups of two or three,
behaving as a whole,
would seem to make a case for me
for intertwining souls.

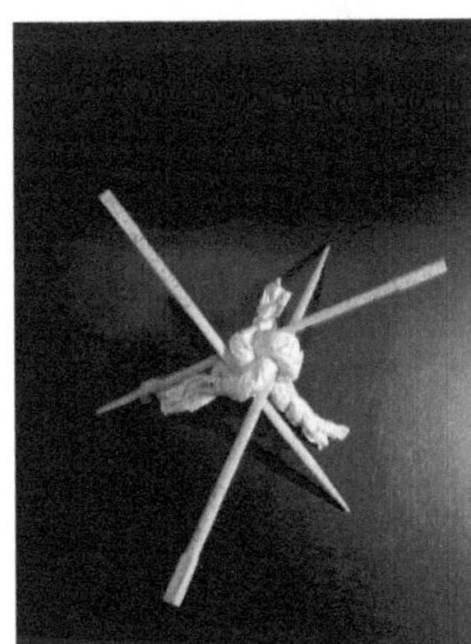

QUANTUM ENTANGLED GHZ TRIPLET
Helaman Ferguson, 2014
Sculpted for Sandy Coleman
from chopsticks and paper napkins

A point in space begins to move
creating endpoints – clearly two!
A new dimension is defined,
as point evolves into a line.
This segment, we shall call an edge,
and on its motion now will hedge
the growth of what we call a face,
as likewise edge a path doth trace.
But note, the path's particular.
It must be perpendicular!
So, long before the face is through,
of matching edges there are two!
Two others grow as we progress,
but two are instantaneous!
With length that equals width attained,
we change the way we move again,
and, once more, right away, it's clear,
two matching faces just appear.
Four more develop over time,
but two are instantly defined!
Extending to the hypercube,
assuming a new way to move,
the cube, which has six matching faces,
a path analogous now traces,
where slightest motion yields in full
two separate cubes – identical!
These move apart in such a fashion,
their pathway we can scarce imagine,
but, by analogy, in time,

six other cubes will be defined.
At this point, what results we call
a cube that's four dimensional.
There's nothing special about four.
There could be any number more.
We try within our space to learn
to see them through the twists and turns
and slices that don't show the whole,
but, rather, how the form unfolds.
But always, it would seem to me,
the thing most difficult to see
is that small speck of space and time,
where separateness is first defined!

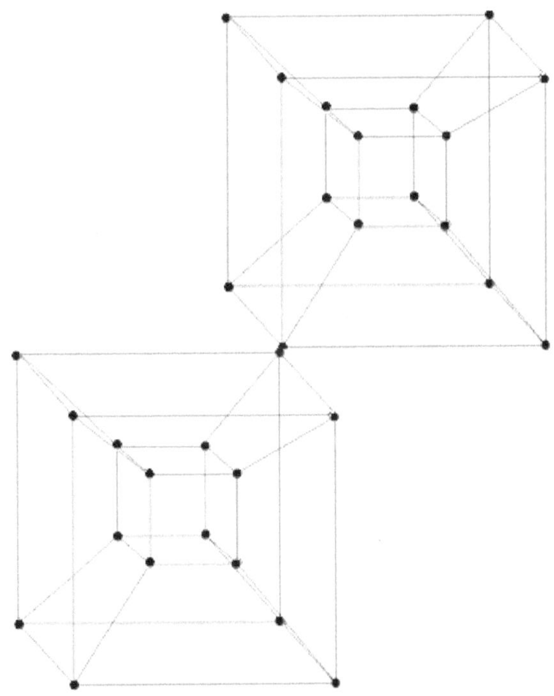

Time is a tangle of twisted curves,
except for Eigen-time,
which, oddly, human beings observe
as moving in a line,
extending to infinities
so far beyond our grasp
that whether time begins or ends
it seems a waste to ask.
We're living in the here and now,
whatever that may be,
in order that we may, somehow,
define reality.

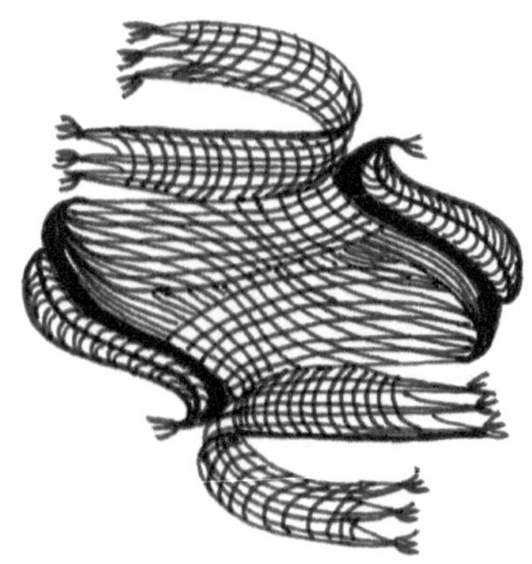

All clocks eventually go lame.
All motion dissipates.
All things return to dust again,
if we but watch and wait.

It may require eternity
for matter to be still,
but there are laws that seem to say,
eventually, it will.

When all's returned to nothingness,
we'll neither know nor care,
since there will be no trace of us
to even be aware.

But will we pass through bits of time
between the now and then,
when we will suddenly divine,
we're not what we have been?

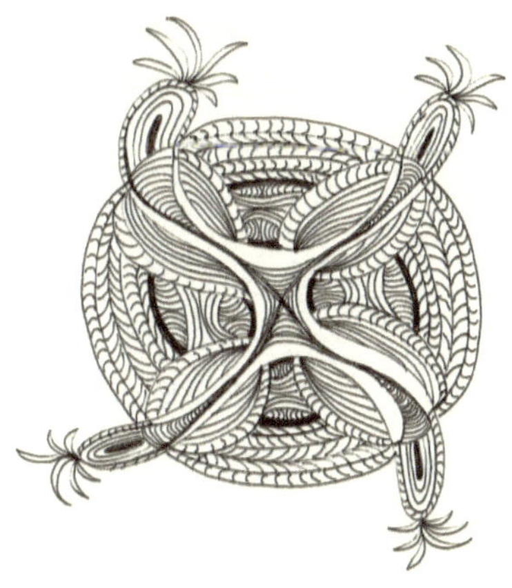

The pleasure I derive from creating a semi-symmetrical drawing lies in the freedom to choose the steps in my own algorithm and the discipline required to follow the rules enough times to produce symmetry. The process brings a calming feeling of order amid chaos. My drawings are different from precise mathematical designs that rely heavily on rulers, compasses, protractors and other tools. I usually use none of these. In this drawing, however, I decided to use one tool—a simple ruler. I wanted the design to fit within the boundaries of a rectangle with an approximate 7:9 ratio of width to length. So, I penciled in a few dots—actually a lot of dots. Then I created the piece by connecting the dots with hand-drawn curves and imagery.

In this design, both obvious and hidden images suggest my frame of mind as I worked to connect the dots. Because personal psychology and life experiences so affect the ways different people may connect any given set of dots, it is certain that a hundred different people, given this same set of dots, would likely connect the dots in a hundred different ways—even if all were looking to follow a set of rules—even if all were hoping to find calm in the midst of chaos. A hundred different people might also see in my connected curves and imagery a hundred different stories and foresee a hundred different endings to a mathematical fairy tale woven of patterns repeating themselves.

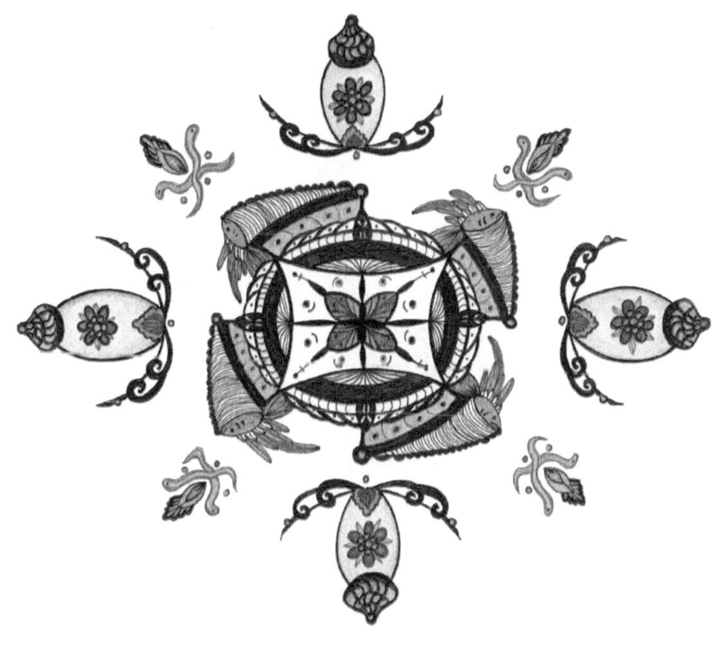

CONNECTING THE DOTS
20" x 24"
Ink and Graphite on Paper
2019

A point with zero edges, faces
is, oh! so very small!
In fact, the vertex, in this case, is
nothing much at all!

Still, a point can trace a path, you see,
that we would call a line,
where, suddenly, two vertices
and one edge we would find.

Now, if the line should trace in Space
a figure – then it's clear –
four vertices, four edges, and one face
would then appear.

This new form, moving forward,
at right angles to itself,
would trace a cube, and, what is more,
I've noticed something else!

With six faces and eight vertices,
twelve edges counted now,
there ought to be a pattern we
could figure out, somehow!

The vertices, it seems to me,
go 1, 2, 4, and 8...
To say 16 should follow these
I'd scarcely hesitate.

For the edge count – 0, 1, 4, 12...
the pattern seems to be
to add to twice the previous term
the previous vertices.

So, if we want to figure out
the number next in line,
to double twelve and add an eight
it seems will work just fine!

The face count would seem hard to do
with 0, 0, 1 and 6....
But – if you think about it – you
could use the same old trick.

Except, for each successive term,
to twice the term before,
we add the previous edges,
so that, next comes 24!

Could we but think of a direction
that our minds could clearly see
as being perpendicular
to x and y and z –

the cube could trace a figure, too,
and we'd see then with our eyes,
the hypercube that, now, our minds
can only analyze!

*In response to Helaman Ferguson's challenge to extend the
concept in rhyme to n-dimensional hypercubes*

A point with zero edges, faces
is, oh! so very small!
In fact, the vertex, in this case, is
nothing much at all!

Still, a point can trace a path, you see,
that we would call a line,
where, suddenly, two vertices
and one edge we would find.

Now, if the line should trace in Space
a figure – then it's clear –
four vertices, four edges, and one face
would then appear.

This new form, moving forward,
at right angles to itself,
would trace a cube, and, what is more,
I've noticed something else!

With six faces and eight vertices,
twelve edges counted now,
there ought to be a pattern we
could figure out, somehow!

The vertices, it seems to me,
go 1, 2, 4, and 8...
To say 16 should follow these
I'd scarcely hesitate.

For the edge count – 0, 1, 4, 12...
the pattern seems to be
to add to twice the previous term
the previous vertices.

So, if we want to figure out
the number next in line,
to double twelve and add an eight
it seems will work just fine!

The face count would seem hard to do
with 0, 0, 1 and 6....
But – if you think about it – you
could use the same old trick.

Except, for each successive term,
to twice the term before,
we add the previous edges,
so that, next comes 24!

Could we but think of a direction
that our minds could clearly see
as being perpendicular
to x and y and z –
the cube could trace a figure, too,
and we'd see then with our eyes,
the hypercube that, now, our minds
can only analyze!

If we give these numbers careful thought,
it seems we might deduce,
that there's a pattern overall
that we could put to use.

If we labeled all the hypercubes
in terms of n's and d's,
beginning, now, with "zero-cubes"
instead of "vertices,"

And called the lines the "one-cubes,"
and let "two-cubes" mean the squares,
what we mean by saying "n-cube,"
I should think would be quite clear.

Then, if the *n*-cubes grow from *d*-cubes
in the way that we have shown,
it would seem that there's a pattern
that goes on and on and on.

If we assign to all the lesser
hypercubes dimension *d,*
we could count within the *n*-cube
all the lesser cubes, you see.

For if
$0 \le d \le n,$
We find
$$\binom{n}{d} * 2^{n-d}$$
yields those very same numbers again!

That this pattern would continue
seems apparent at this time,
but please don't ask me to display
the proof in metered rhyme!

vertices	edges	faces	cubes	hypercubes	5-cubes
0-cubes	1-cubes	2-cubes	3-cubes	4-cubes	5-cubes
$d=0$	$d=1$	$d=2$	$d=3$	$d=4$	$d=5$
1	0	0	0	0	0
2	1	0	0	0	0
4	4	1	0	0	0
8	12	6	1	0	0
16	32	24	8	1	0
32	80	80	40	10	1
64	192	240	160	60	12

It seems that we *could* find a proof
without a great production.
Indeed, would it not follow
from a double math induction?
We have a basis, clear enough,
for either *n* or *d.*
Let's keep *d* fixed and vary *n*
and see where that would lead...
Or keep *n* fixed and vary *d*...
However we proceed, would we
not get the same result –
a kind of symmetry?

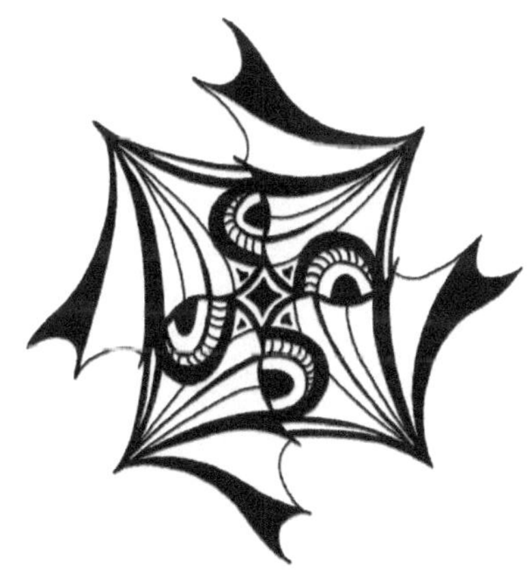

Two trains that passed
on parallel tracks,
less alone in
each other's light,
moved along so fast
that on looking back
there was only
another night
But two souls that peered
from the moving cars,
caught a glimpse
of familiar eyes—
and it seemed so clear
that it pierced their hearts.
as their destinies passed them by.

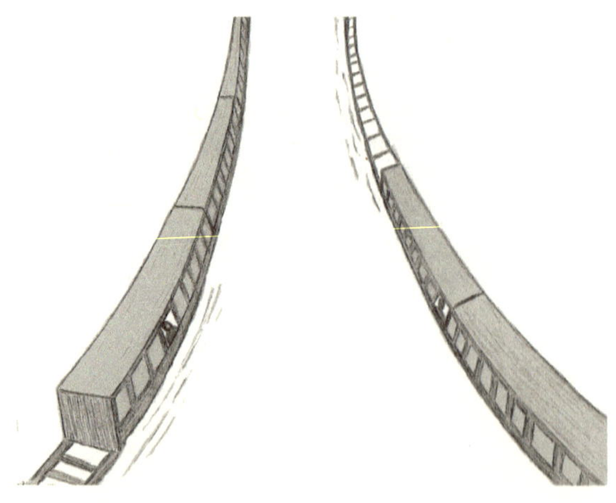

The universe unfolds itself in multiplicity.
That this is true a host of modern scientists agree.
What I perceive as here and now can scarcely be defined,
if there are many here and nows completely intertwined.
Am I completely in this space? Or am I elsewhere, too?
And, could there really be a place where I am still with you?

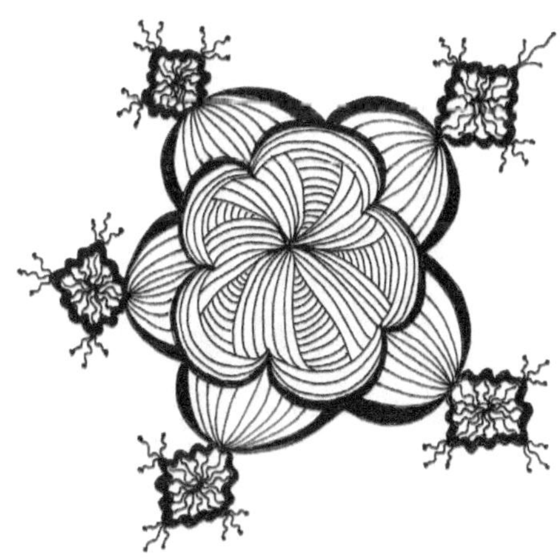

If the sum of all the angles
in a shape upon a sphere
exceeds the sum which on a
planar surface would appear,
why base the count of polytopes
in all the n dimensions
upon the angles we can join
in three-space? By convention?

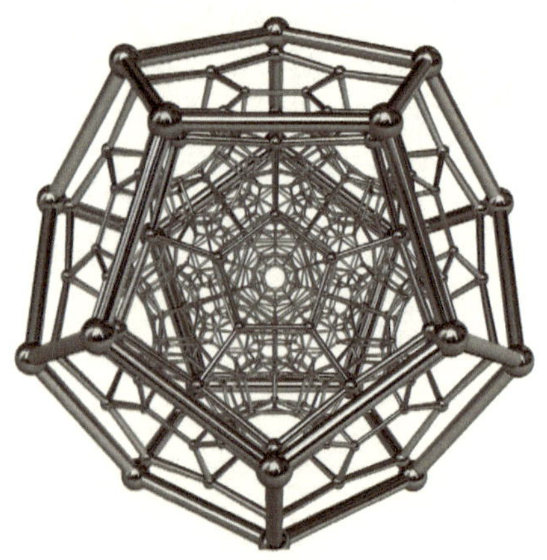

120-cell Schlegel wireframe
Robert Webb of Stella software
http://www.software3d.com/Stella.php

I saw a blackbird spread her wings
and float upon the air –
not flying, just gliding,
without a thought or care.
And on the front porch, near the swing,
a rose bush, growing there,
has roses in hiding
it very soon will share.

The children coming home from school
are laughing as they pass –
enjoying the sunshine –
walking barefoot in the grass.
There ought to be some sort of rule –
but there is none, alas –
declaring that in springtime
it is legal to skip class.

I understand more clearly
the language of the birds
than some attempts to reach me
through symbols framed in words.
Though birds have no intention
to touch or change my soul,
they move me with the music
of a certain joy they know –
the joy that thrives on freedom,
on being one with air,
so unimpaired by reason,
so unconstrained by care.

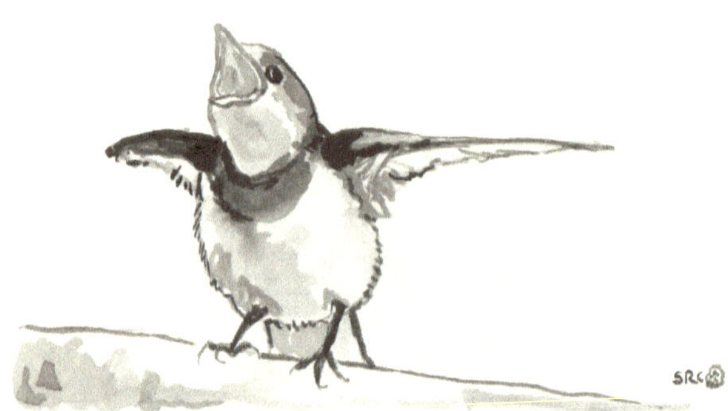

The birds I hear singing make sweet melody –
make their messages lovely and long.
Why would you insist there can only be three
different notes in a warbler's song?

The birds I hear singing have so much to say,
as they chirp from their twigs in the tree,
that try as they may there is really no way
that their notes could be kept to just three.

The birds I hear singing sweet mysteries would tell –
so much more than you've let yourself hear.
You might be quite surprised, if you'd just listen well
to their songs as they fall on your ear.

The birds I hear singing from morning 'til night,
by the light of the sun and the moon,
have been known, as a fact, to make use of their right
to start singing a different tune.

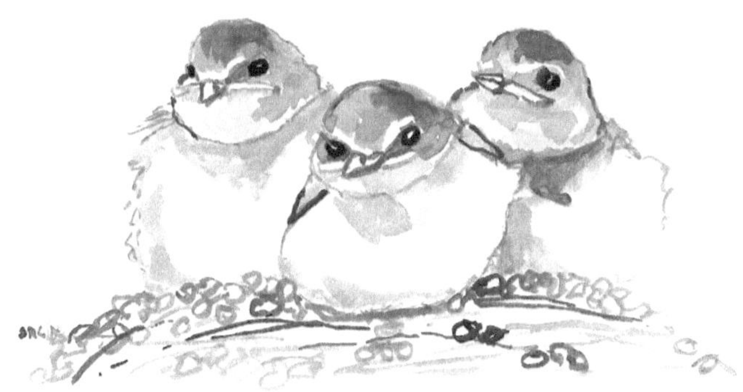

I know the songs of cardinals, of mourning doves, of crows,
but one is very often wrong in what one thinks one knows.

The cardinal, who so often pays his compliments to me,
today left off his pretty song and spoke more quietly.
In gentle, but insistent, strains, in unfamiliar tweets,
he seemed to say that life abounds in treasures soft and sweet.

The crow's familiar "Caw! Caw! Caw!" he sang as usual,
but added in between the calls a song more beautiful.
I might have thought he could not sing such dovelike gentle song,
but then, as in so many things, my thinking would be wrong.

The mourning dove, as yet, has sung but one sweet song to me,
the lonesome echo through the wood he voices, constantly.
But there is more to every soul than one sweet song can sing,
and glimpses of the hidden whole are caught by listening.

Today, as plain as any sound that I have ever heard,
sprang wholly unfamiliar songs from most familiar birds.

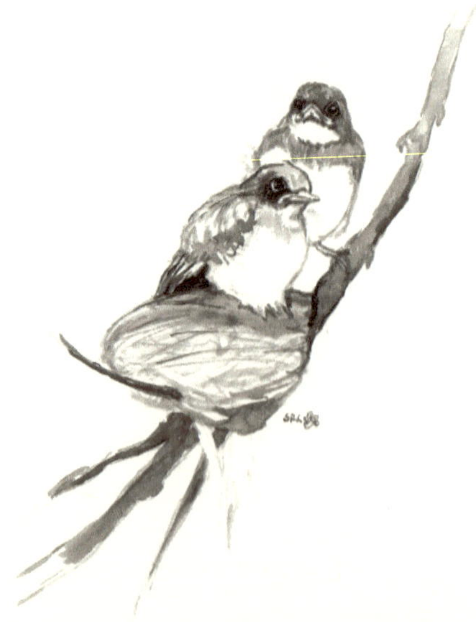

This was my father's book.
The comments in the margins in his hand,
tell me he read and tried to understand
Wordsworth and Keats and Shelley and the rest.
I see what pains he took
to capture the heart of each immortal line.
I see and yet I know not his design.
Perhaps to make a grade. Perhaps a quest –
a well-planned, careful look
for words which might express or change his mind.
At any rate, I'm very glad to find
we've shared some thoughts some souls might call the best.

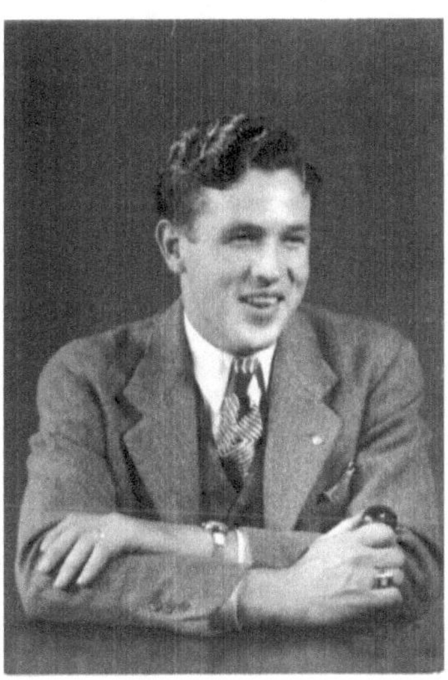

MILTON E. DeLozier (1924-1957)

You may not be a Longfellow, a Byron, or a Keats.
You may not show what's in your mind with great poetic feats.
But, if you even try to reach my heart from time to time
by showing what's inside of you, or part of it, in rhyme,
the try will move me more than you can possibly imagine,
for I have learned in poems to read life's tenderness and passion.
In verse, there is a voice unheard that's hidden in the flow,
and meter adds to spoken words what prose can never show.
A heart that's burdened, overfilled with love or fear or joy
finds sweet expression if it will the art of rhyme employ.

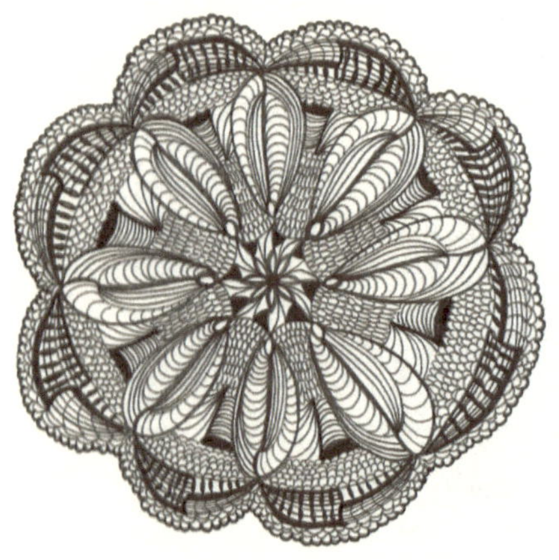

I asked my love to send a poem.
I hoped that I would find
words that would show to me his heart –
the thoughts that fill his mind.
I'd hoped that he would write his own,
but said it would be fine,
if he sent one that touched his heart.
He sent back one of mine.

We are forever immersed in patterns of symmetry, whether seen or unseen. We can find countless examples of symmetry in the everyday world around us – in flowers, in fruits and vegetables and in the growth patterns of tiny seedlings. We are a little less likely to be aware of the symmetry and certain mathematical beauty in the microscopic inhabitants of our environment. A search for magnified images of viruses and vitamins reveals a fascinating hidden world in which a host of structures display near-perfect symmetry.

The inspiration for this drawing was a set of images displaying more directly a study of developing, dynamic symmetry. The September 2016 issue of PHYSICS TODAY describes an experiment designed to increase our understanding of proportionate growth. By observing the flow patterns associated with displacement of higher viscosity fluids by fluids of lower viscosity, the researchers hoped to connect their observations to questions concerning biological growth, such as the question of why body parts grow at nearly the same rate, maintaining direct proportion to one another.

I began my drawing by mimicking the pattern of growth of one off-shoot of a symmetrically spreading fluid and from there created my own symmetry through unmeasured algorithmic repetitions. It is interesting to me that, although no living organism was the model for the art, my young granddaughter says it is a drawing of autumn leaves.

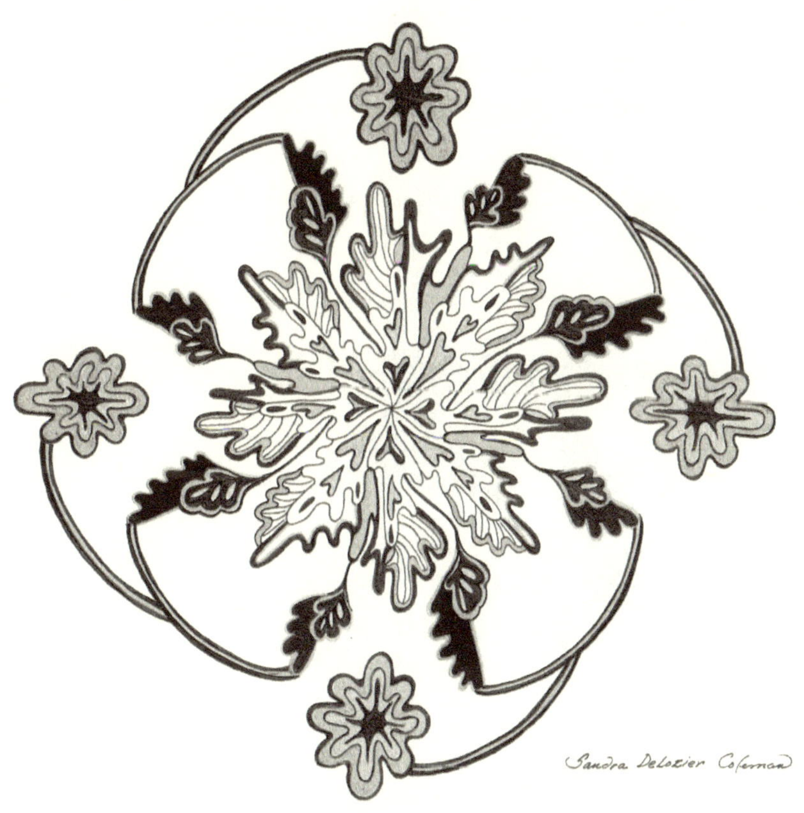

Autumn Leaves
20" x 20"
Ink on paper
2016

Sure Shelley was wise and an ancient soul.
For these words of wisdom may he be praised,
who said, if thy mistress some anger shows,
imprison her hand and let her rave,
and feed deep, deep on her peerless eyes.
Would that all men should be so wise!

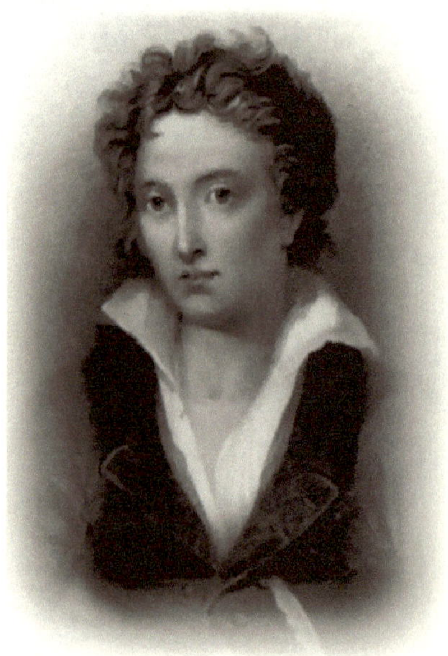

PERCY BYSSHE SHELLEY (1792-1822)

A poet whose clear legacy
is illusiveness of form,
obscurity of image,
vision different from the norm,
with a quiet sense of order
beneath mystery unfurled,
reveals that he is sorting out,
a most confusing world.

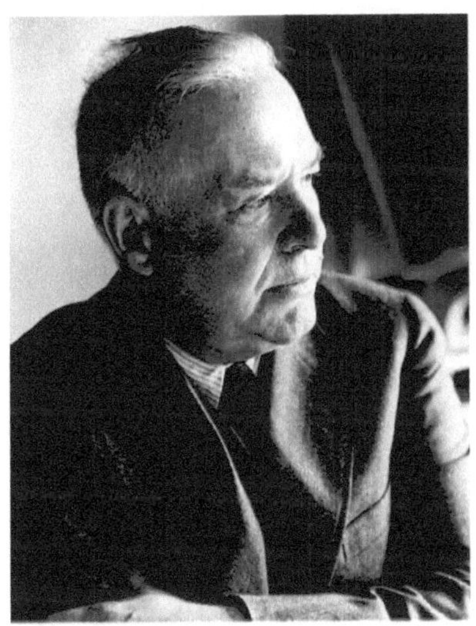

WALLACE STEVENS (1879-1955)

Surrounded as I am, no doubt,
by scholars, poets, analysts, and friends
of one whose poems have been sought out
and read and read and read again by them.
I realize his claim to fame,
the source of his appeal,
is that his poems provide a game
at guessing what he feels.
Ambiguous words he strings along
to tantalize the ear,
but just what motivates his song
is often quite unclear.
Still, scholars from the world around
convening to share clues,
announce with pride that they have found
what others say they knew!

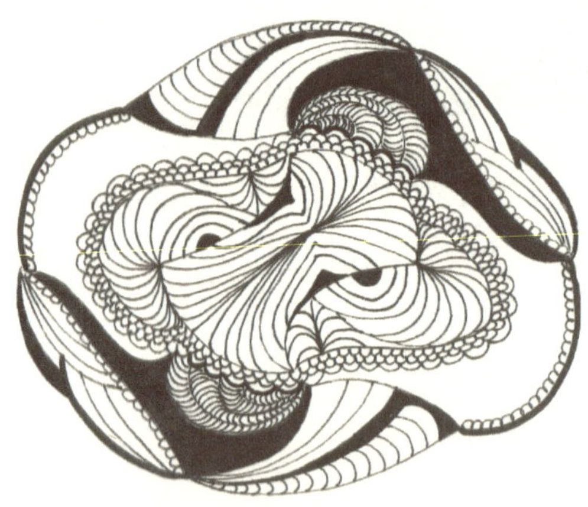

THIRTEEN WAYS OF LOOKING AT A RED LEAF

(IN THE PATTERN OF WALLACE STEVENS)

I

Among a hundred swaying branches,
The only thing of color
Was the red leaf of the maple.

II

I hold three thoughts,
A limpid pool
In which three red leaves are floating.

III

The red leaf cupped to hold the morning dew.
It was both joy and duty.

IV

A life and a death
Are one.
A life and a death and a red leaf
Are one.

V

I do not know which to prefer,
The mettle of tenacity
Or the joy of abandon,
The red leaf clinging
Or falling.

VI
A mass of watery, heavy leaves
Covers the tree at the roots.
The recently fallen leaf
Flies to and fro.
The choices –
To merge with the others below
Or to yearn for the others above.

VII
O man of reclusion and reason,
Why live a life of enigmas?
Do you not see in the leaf
Of the maple the hair
Of a woman you loved?

VIII
I know automaton
And the volatility of dreams;
But I know, too,
That the red leaf is involved
In what I know.

IX
When the red leaf flutters to the ground,
This is a dance,
Un-choreographed effusion.

X

At the sight of red leaves
In pattern in blue sky,
Even modernists
Find lucidity in lyric.

XI

She wintered in Connecticut
And her looking glass,
Once, in a brief moment,
Returned, by some mistake
A hint in her reflection
Of red leaf.

XII

The frost is forming.
The red leaf must be dying.

XIII

It was autumn all summer.
It was sunless
And it was going to be sunless.
The small bird
Sang within and of red leaves.

Someone famous, I recall,
from a rose thorn prick did fall,
and, if I remember right,
he did die that very night.
Was it Rilke, tender bard,
who, so, by a rose was scarred?
Mystical, mysterious end
to one who once a poem penned
that, though borrowed, pierced my heart,
deep as any deadly dart.

You, Who Never Confessed

(IN THE PATTERN OF RANIER MARIE RILKE)

You, who never confessed
one small need, Beloved, who were silent
from when we began,
I don't even know what verses have moved you.
I have given up guessing
which image you show me
is real. All that inspires emotion and longing –
the sea, the blackberry, the wind in my hair –
appear as mere aspects of you –
you, who know not who you are.

You, the once loved, whom I called
to my gardens, and gazed on as though
you were all I could need. Through side streets
of countries that seemed so familiar, I've looked
for the image of all we could be.
Beside me in spirit, where e'er I have traveled,
as though nothing mattered that we had not shared.
Sometimes, still, in brief moments too fleeting, I capture
a glimpse of the tender and modest, the boy,
whom my poems about love, like the notes of the wood thrush,
revived, and once offered a promise of joy.

Le Capitaine Sans Coeur

(In the Pattern of John Keats)

I

O WHAT can ail thee, maid so fair
Alone and wandering aimlessly?
The waves still wash upon the shore,
But there's no sea.

II

O what can ail thee, maid so fair!
So weary and bereft of sun?
The sailors have come sailing home.
The journey's done.

III

I see a cloud upon thy face
Thine eyes a mix of mist and rain,
And on thy lips a rainbow curve,
That speaks of pain.

IV

I met a captain like the sea,
A handsome man – with bluest eyes,
His hair was thick and black and curled.
His voice, it mesmerized.

V

I made a cushion for his heart,
And comforter of softest down
He took the gifts as gifts of love,
With ne'er a frown.

VI

I climbed aboard his mighty ship,
And sought no other vessel fair,
For oft the songs he sang to me
Did fill the air.

VII

He gathered shell fish from the sea,
And with them did my hunger feed,
And I am sure I heard him say –
"It's you I need."

VIII

He took me to an island hut,
And there he wept, and held me long,
And there I fed his hungriness
And sang him songs.

IX

And there he lulled me into trust,
And there I dreamed – Ah! Painful sight! –
The dream that haunts me every day
And every night.

X

I saw a white-winged heavenly host,
In sorrow for me were they all;
They cried, "Alas, the Lord of Lies
Hath thee in thrall!"

XI

I saw their eyes so full of love,
With horror looking on my fate.
Then I awoke and found me here,
Beyond their gate.

XII

And this is why I linger here,
Alone and wandering aimlessly.
Though waves still wash upon the shore,
There is no sea.

(Based on Sonnets from the Portuguese, Elizabeth Barrett Browning)

I.   Love sprung upon my heart with power that made me new.
    There is no all of me without that best part – you.

VII.   And every part of life which I hold dear,
    has meaning for me only when you're near.

X.   You call me beautiful, for you
    see only what I feel because of you

XII.   And even this one beauty free
    belongs to you and really not to me.

XIV.   No part of me deserves the love you give;
    so love for love's sake that our love may live,

XV.   Forgiving if I seem to fear sometimes
    the very love that makes all beauty mine.

XVI.   As sunlight dries up all the heaven's tears,
    the strength of your love vanishes my fears.

XX.   I wonder how I passed through twenty springs,
    not knowing of the joy that true love brings.

XXI.   You love me, love me say it once again.
    I drink the words as flowers drink the rain.

XXII.   We sit and gaze together though apart;
    I feel love's blanket soft about my heart.

XXIV.   Though pain and sorrow knock upon our door,
    as long as we have love we are not poor.

XXV.   When childish fears have left me in despair,
    your calm, firm love removes my every care.

XXVI.   The visions that had filled my girlish mind
    for twenty sunlit summers now behind

XXVII.   Held nothing in their sunlight to compare
    to love like ours, so beautiful – so rare.

XXIX.   My dreams were very beautiful indeed,
    but full-blown dreams are but a true love's seed.

WHEN WILL I LEAVE THEE

(IN THE PATTERN OF ELIZABETH BARRETT BROWNING)

When will I leave thee? It will not be soon!
I'll be here 'til the sun no longer shines
Upon the earth, or 'til the time
Her light's no more reflected in the moon.
I'll be here 'til December mates with June
And all the stars of heaven, with their signs
For all the seasons, so combine
That we may see both snow and rose in bloom!
I'll be here through the slowest passing days –
Through those that course like light in stormy skies.
I'll be here when all others pass away –
Endeavoring, love, for your sake not to die,
As long as you have need to have me stay
or, with you, 'neath the earth, to have me lie.

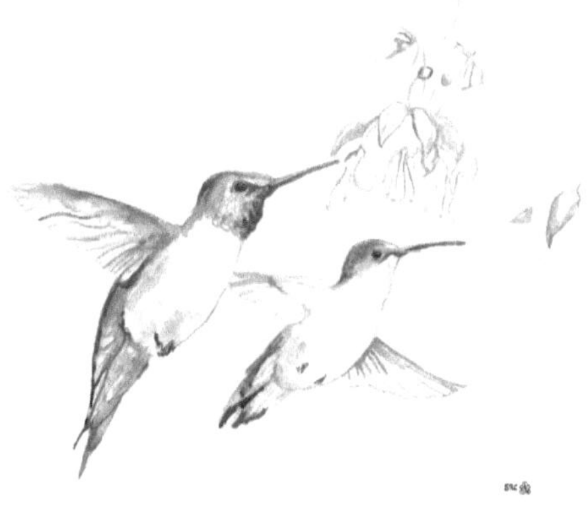

MATH TABLES TURNED

(IN THE PATTERN OF WILLIAM WORDSWORTH)

UP! Up! My Friend, and quit your math;
Or surely you'll grow old:
Up! Up! My Friend, let's have a laugh;
Why must you be so cold?

The moon, above the ocean black,
A mystic orb is shimmering,
As waves wash o'er the shore and back
Beneath its pale light glimmering.

Math! 'tis a dull and endless strife:
Come, hear the crickets chirping.
How sweet they sing their song of life,
Their joy ne'er ours usurping

And listen to the seagull's cry!
He, too, us joy is giving:
Come let us give their dance a try,
And learn the art of living.

For nature has a wondrous way,
Of bringing joy and peace –
A kind of wisdom in her play,
That study can't release.

 One walk upon a sandy shore
Beneath a lunar glow,
Of what should count may teach you more,
Than all the Math you know.

Sweet were the hours in Nature's school,
Should we but students stay
Immersed enough to learn the rules
That guide us every day.

Enough of Math! Now close your book;
No more these problems ponder.
Come listen, taste and touch and look;
The world is full of wonder!

TO CORNBERG

These are my poems!
They are not yours!
How dare you interfere
and try to force
into my verse
the fashion of the year!

It's who I am
and what I feel
and what I want to say!
If you can't give
your precious seal,
then, please, just stay away!

These are my thoughts
and mine alone!
They may not fit your mold!
I'm sure that rhyming
will go on
when this year's style is old!

I like the sound
of metered rhyme,
the pattern and the plan
and, if I changed
a single line,
I'd make it rhyme again!

A LASS, ALAS

Please, sir, I heard
you vow just now
to wed yon pretty lass.
Her smile beguiles.
Oh! How I know!
But please, sir, let it pass!

Her song and long
thick hair I dare
say charmed much stronger men,
but none have won
her heart, and smart
men never try again.

I've seen her mean
enough to snuff
the very flames of hell!
And sir, I've heard
such stories! Lo!
I'd be ashamed to tell!

Her eyes tell lies
and with her kiss
she captivates the soul.
I'm told she holds
twelve now! I vow
her heart's as black as coal!

Twelve lads who've had
a taste and waste
their lives in seeking more!

I ask, Is that
a thing to sing?
I swear she's keeping score!

Please, sir, confer
with any man
who lives within this town.
He'll say today
without a doubt
It's best to settle down.

Let pass this lass
who's arms and charms
have caused so many strife.
Now, tarry, marry
if you must. Just
choose some other wife

Who'll sit and knit
and bake you cakes
and keep your covers warm,
A maid who'll stay
your wife for life
and never do you harm.

But of this one miss,
I do say true,
it's best to let her be!
For the man who can
make her defer
is a better man than me!

A CADDISH LAD

Fair maid you said
a vow just now
to win yon laddie's heart.
Now, though I know
he's armed with charms,
that plan would not be smart.

He'll smile the while
he hurls a girl
a compliment or two,
but words you heard
him say today
tomorrow won't be true.

He lures the pure
and fair to care,
but love he won't return.
His heart is hard.
His mind unkind,
and many he hath spurned.

He'll coo to you
and sing such things,
you're sure to think him nice,
but then just when
he's sparked your heart
his own will turn to ice.

Don't choose to lose
your innocence
to one not worth the risk.

You see, 't would be
a great mistake
to taste this devil's kiss.

No lass he has,
yet, loved enough
to give his heart away,
and all who fall
will meet defeat
and live to rue the day.

I gave a knave,
a caddish lad,
a love he bought with lies.
I'm here, my dear,
to steer you clear
of choices so unwise.

Maid, find the kind
of man who can
be loved and love return.
Don't make mistakes
when from someone
her lesson you can learn.

Resist his kiss
and flea his plea.
Lass! Find some other man!
For she whom he
hath charmed I warn
shall never love again.

THE NIGHT BEFORE FINALS

(IN THE PATTERN OF CLEMENT CLARKE MOORE)

'Twas the night before finals and all through the house
Not a pencil was stirring. We were all studied out!
Our class notes were laid on the table with care,
In hopes that the answers we needed were there.
We were brushing our teeth and preparing for bed,
Though problems and formulas crowded our heads.
We'd taken as much as we could of that math,
And were just settling down for a much-needed nap,
When out on the lawn we heard such a clatter,
I jumped out of bed to see what was the matter.
Holding my breath, and clutching my heart,
Away to the window I flew like a dart.
The moon in the clear winter sky shone so bright
We had closed all the curtains to shut out the light.
Now, what to my horrified eyes should appear,
But a miniature sleigh, and eight tiny reindeer,
With a little math teacher, so lively and quick,
I felt right away I was going to be sick.
As quick as computers her courses they came,
And she whistled, and shouted, and called them by name:
"Now, Algebra! Finite! Stats! PreCalc! and Trig!
On Business Calc! Calc! Diffe-thing-a-ma-gig!
To the top of the class! To the top of the line!
Study! study! and study! and all will be fine!"
As trees in wild hurricanes swagger and sway,
'Til their trunks are uprooted and finally give way,
With more wind force than Opal, she prodded that crew,
'Til up to the house-top the eight reindeer flew.

With the force of a tree trunk that lands on the roof
She landed up there with her bag full of proofs.
We'd locked up the windows and doors all around,
But right down the chimney she came with a bound.
She had dressed up for work, the way most teachers do,
But I saw on her face little smudges of blue;
A bundle of books she had flung on her back,
Suggesting we give those books one final whack.
Her eyes – how they twinkled! They sparkled and shone!
We could see right away she was not going home!
Her plan was determined – her mind-set was clear!
There'd be no failing grades on her final this year!
A SHARP calculator she held in her fist,
As she looked at the time on the watch on her wrist;
She had a kind face, even I must admit,
So I gave in and looked for a good place to sit.
It was clear she was going to be there a while,
So I figured I might as well listen and smile.
She spoke a few words, then with marker in hand,
She worked problems for hours on a board on a stand;
Then laying her finger aside of her nose,
And giving a nod, up the chimney she rose;
She sprang to her sleigh, to her team gave a holler,
And away they all flew like my last hard-earned dollar.
But I heard her exclaim as her team flew away,
"Happy finals to all, and to all a good grade!"

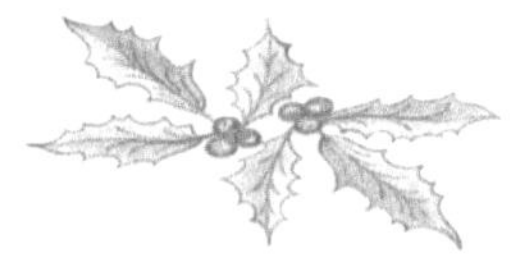

THE TWO-HEADED GIANT

Long, long ago in a land far away,
where fairies and giants appear every day,
lived a two-headed giant, enormous and strong,
who, alas, with himself just could not get along.
His left mind loved numbers. His right mind loved art.
And it seems they had each felt this way from the start.
The left studied science. The right preferred plays.
They fought about spending their money for days!
They could only keep mealtime from being a riot
by letting each head have a separate diet.
The left head liked bland food. The right head liked spice –
though at times they agreed something sweet might be nice.
But after the treat the left brain was in pain,
while the right couldn't wait to have sugar again.
And we won't spend much time on details of digestion –
You can probably imagine from just a suggestion.
Whenever the giant felt dizzy and queasy,
deciding just who should be sick wasn't easy.
In fact, I've been told that the giant's been seen
lying down in the woods with both heads rather green!
As if learning to eat weren't enough of a worry,
one side liked to dawdle, the other to hurry.
Their compromise skills had become such a wreck
that each outing they took was a pain in the neck!
Even sleeping was not a relief to the fellow,
since both liked to sleep with an arm 'neath a pillow,
and the giant had never quite mastered the knack
of falling asleep with two heads back-to-back.
They would never take turns, though it had been suggested,
and so the poor giant was never quite rested.
Though his problems were many, you can see from these few,
he would have to do something, but what could he do?

The solution, at first, neither head seemed to know,
but, at last, it was clear that one head had to GO!
But who would decide which of them it should be,
since they seldom, if ever, were known to agree.
They went to a wizard they'd heard was quite wise,
who could read people's thoughts by the looks in their eyes.
Being known for his wisdom throughout the whole kingdom,
they both thought it best to let him choose between them.
The wizard, accustomed to fairies and goblins,
showed the giant right in, asking what was the problem.
He offered the sturdiest chair he could find,
then he told each to say what he had on his mind.
As horses jump in at the start of a race,
each started to shout and to offer his case!
Before the poor wizard could let out a "Whoa!"
each head had said more than he needed to know.
He knew in a flash, he would have to use magic,
or the poor giant's fate would be nothing but tragic.
He pulled out his wand, gave his spell book a glance,
and proceeded to put the right head in a trance.
He then told the left head to be on his way,
unless he had something he wanted to say.
You'd think there'd be something the left head would mention,
on finding he had undivided attention,
but the words didn't seem to make sense, anymore.
So, he just turned around and walked out of the door.
As he walked down the road that led back to his home,
he tried to get used to this being alone.
It seemed rather strange, though, to go for a walk
with no one to hear if he started to talk.
Though he noticed a beautiful bird on the wing,
he knew that the right head had not seen a thing.

The flowers he saw by the road everywhere,
now seemed so much less lovely with no one to share.
Back home, he was hungry. He made up a meal.
It was bland like he liked, but without much appeal.
At bedtime, he thought he'd at least get some rest,
but could not fall asleep, though, he gave it his best.
It seems he'd grown used to the sound of a snore,
and without it he just couldn't sleep, anymore.
He finally rose with a stretch and a yawn,
and waited and watched for the coming of dawn.
Next day, the poor giant to the wizard returned
to tell him he thought that his lesson he'd learned.
He told him that being alone was no fun
and that two heads were truly much better than one.
To the wizard, it seems, this was not a surprise.
He commanded the right head to open his eyes.
Delighted to be taken out of his trance,
he woke up so happy, he started to dance.
The left head, at first, was inclined to resist,
but soon he just sighed and said, "If you insist!"
I can't quite imagine, but, still, I've been told,
that the dance that ensued was a sight to behold!
The wizard applauded. The heads took a bow
and promised they'd work out their problems somehow.
The two heads left smiling and sharing their thoughts
and getting along, the way all people ought.
Ever since, they've been working together in sync.
Now, there's nothing too hard for this giant to think.
The moral, it seems, should be clear beyond doubt.
The left brain, the right brain cannot do without.

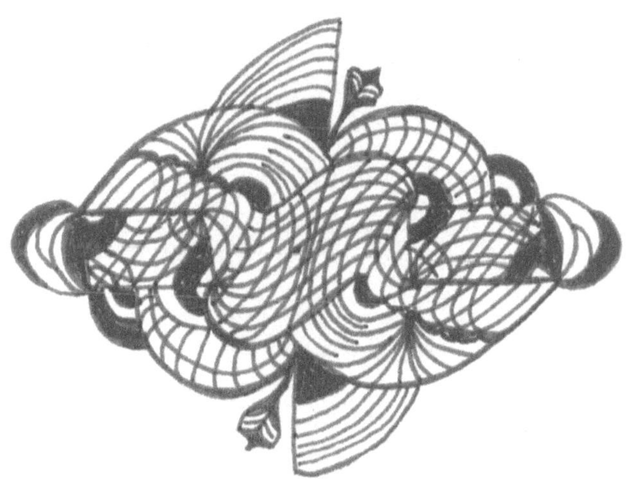

www.ingramcontent.com/pod-product-compliance
Lightning Source LLC
Chambersburg PA
CBHW031047160726
47991CB00005B/2050